Bioinformatics and Bioprogramming in C

L N CHAVALI
Visiting faculty, Osmania University
Hyderabad

Universities Press

Universities Press (India) Private Limited

Registered Office
3-6-747/1/A & 3-6-754/1, Himayatnagar, Hyderabad 500 029 (A.P.), India
E-mail: *info@universitiespress.com*

Distributed by
Orient Blackswan Private Limited

Registered Office
3-6-752, Himayatnagar, Hyderabad 500 029 (A.P.), India

Other Offices
Bangalore / Bhopal / Bhubaneshwar / Chennai
Ernakulam / Guwahati / Hyderabad / Jaipur / Collate
Lucknow / Mumbai / New Delhi / Patna

First published 2009
Reprinted 2010

Cover and book design

ISBN: 978 81 7371 648 5

Set in Life BT 11/13 by
OSDATA, Hyderabad 500 029

Printed at
Graphica Printers
Hyderabad 500 013

Published by
Universities Press (India) Private Limited
3-6-747/1/A & 3-6-754/1, Himayatnagar, Hyderabad 500 029 (A.P), India

Contents

Foreword

The new millennium has kindled a fresh hope in the minds of biologists. The completion of the working draft first and later the complete human genome is a significant landmark in the study of biology. Since June 2000, the genome sequences of many organisms have been completed and many more are in progress. The human genome contains about 3.1 billion base pairs and this feat of mapping it all would have been virtually impossible without the use of computational methods. Thus, biology is being transformed from a laboratory-based science into an information science. The flood of information in genome sequencing projects led to advances in the understanding of basic biological processes, evolutionary tendencies and also in diagnosis and treatment of many human genetic disorders. A stage has come now where the students and scholars of biology cannot study or carry out research in biology without using the tools of computers and bioinformatics.

While many biologists are afraid of computer programming, computer scientists do not know much about biology. Mr. Chavali, the author of this book is a computer scientist—but he has taken up the challenge of understanding a totally-alien subject for him, biology, and solving some of the problems being faced in biological sciences by students and scholars alike. It is a difficult task to organise the knowledge in this field in logical progression and present it in a simple language. 'The easiest things are hardest to be done', says the famous writer Tennyson. Mr. Chavali has made an all out effort in this book to simplify many programs that are complicated and beyond the comprehension of students of biology. Based on his experience as a computer scientist at various organisations, he has tried to introduce many features and solve many practical problems in the easiest manner possible.

Though many books in bioinformatics have been published, we hardly find books on BioC, BioJava and BioPerl that are comprehensible to the students. As far as I know, this is the first and simplest book on bioprogramming concepts in C language written in a lucid style. Many programs that are mentioned and examples that are cited are explicit and need no or little effort to understand. Mr. Chavali has taken up the challenge of training biology students and making them proficient in the bioprogramming concepts of C language. For those who do not know anything about bioinformatics, I am sure this book will enlighten them. The author in this book has dealt with many aspects of bioinformatics and bioprogramming concepts in C language with remarkable clarity and brevity—the hall mark of a true writer. It is not the matter but the treatment that he gives to many concepts and the practical problems he has solved which are worthy of mentioning here.

Some people may know many things but may not comprehend them. Some others may comprehend but fail to express. Those expressed by some, may not be perceived by others. Perhaps, when perception mellows, it grows into conception. Without a strong perception of both biology and computers, no one can even think of venturing into the field of bioinformatics.

I feel that Mr. Chavali has succeeded in his endeavour to make the students of biology understand the concepts of bioprogramming in C language and many practical aspects of basic bioinformatics. I compliment and congratulate Mr. Chavali for this wonderful but painstaking effort.

Prof. P. B. Kavi Kishor
Department of Genetics
Osmania University
Hyderabad
October 2008

Preface

Bioinformatics is an emerging inter-disciplinary research area and is increasingly being used to improve the quality of life. Computers gather, analyse and merge biological data in bioinformatics using programs generated by biologists.

The purpose of this book is to address programming for bioinformatics related problems and get the bio community more familiarised with C as a programming tool to solve their day-to-day problems in the laboratory. It is also hoped that the book will foster fertilisation between theory and practice. *Bioinformatics and Bioprogramming in C* is basically an introductory text offering a clear exposition of the algorithmic principles driving advances in bioinformatics. It strikes a unique balance between rigorous mathematics and practical techniques, emphasising the ideas underlying algorithms rather than offering a collection of apparently unrelated problems.

This book assumes no previous programming background or exposure whatsoever. Students and scholars from various disciplines or experience can easily feel the uniqueness and richness of C language.

The programming language C was originally developed by Dennis Ritchie of Bell Laboratories and was designed to run on a PDP-11 with a UNIX operating system. It is an excellent language because of the simplicity of expression, the compactness of the code, and the wide range of applicability. Programs in C are structured by variables, arrays or structure declaration and calling functions. The language provides a rich set of operators, and therefore, the programs can be short and efficient. A program written in C will run as fast as one written in assembly language unlike other higher level languages.

At its most basic level, programming simply means telling a computer what to do. The first hard thing about the programming language is learning and becoming comfortable with it. But we know that the best way to learn a new 'human' language is to listen and speak it right from the beginning, without paying too much attention to the grammar. In the same way, to learn the C language, one must start writing C programs. That is just what this book helps in.

It is presented in 11 chapters beginning with the most basic concepts of C; and takes you up to the highest level of C programming including the usually intimidating concepts of pointers, structures, and dynamic allocation. The first nine chapters cover the fundamental terminology, language basic features and essentials needed to understand and write programs in C. The tenth chapter explains the various data structures and their usage in biological applications. The case studies presented in the last chapter discusses in detail real-time biological problems, using some well known algorithms and techniques in bioinformatics. It gives an in-depth understanding of how to derive solutions to real-time problems. The solutions in the section can be scaled up if required; it can even be built as a library of functions for reuse in other biological applications.

Although exercises have not been provided in this edition, subsequent editions will carry a large number of problems at the end of each chapter. Certain advanced features of C language like unions, 1's and 2's complement, register shifting, function pointer implementation and bitwise operations may also be covered in the coming editions.

All the programs presented in this book are compiled and executed using Turbo C compiler for MSDOS. The appendix provides files that have been used in some of the programs in this book. It also lists the most commonly used built-in function calls. It is recommended that the reader enter each program in Turbo C and run the programs to feel the power of C language.

Special care and attention has been taken to see that most of the programs in this book are bio oriented. This book can also be used as a tutorial to students with a biological background. It is highly recommended that the user go through the chapters in the order presented in the book.

This text has been compiled in collaboration with Prof P. B. Kavi Kishore and Mr. G. Sravan Kumar, an academic consultant at the Bioinformatics Center, Prof. G. Rami Reddy Center for Distance Education, Osmania University.

Acknowledgments

I wish to profoundly thank Prof P. B. Kavi Kishor, former Head, Department of Genetics and currently Chairman, Board of Studies in Genetics, Osmania University, Hyderabad and also Course Coordinator, Bioinformatics at the same University, who initiated and induced me to write this book. *Bioinformatics and Bioprogramming in C* was written to act as a bridge between a computer specialist and a biologist. In fact, Prof Kishor was instrumental in identifying and suggesting certain gaps which required to be filled in the innovative study of bioinformatics. He took keen interest in reviewing the entire work.

I am grateful to Prof A. Subramanyam, Prof and Head, Microbiology and Biotechnology, MIET, Meerut, for introducing me to Prof P. B. Kavi Kishor and for being a constant source of inspiration during the preparation of this book.

My sincere thanks are also due to Ms. Siva Kumari Nunna, Academic Consultant, Bioinformatics Center, Prof. G. Rami Reddy Center for Distance Education, Osmania University for helping me understand the basic terminology and concepts in biology; for screening and testing all the programs in the book; and for providing the necessary inputs and feedback. She spent many hours with me discussing various approaches and ideas and was also kind enough to edit some of the text.

My two lovely children Ram Lohtih and Sriya and my beloved wife, Anitha have been very patient and highly supportive during my preparation of this work. Without their encouragement this book would not have been possible. I acknowledge and appreciate their support and affection.

Laxmi N. Chavali

Introduction

By its simplest definition, bioinformatics is the intersection of information technology and biological sciences. However, as you enter into this grey area, you will soon find that 'bioinformatics' is a fuzzy word meaning different things to different groups of researchers or even when used in different contexts. Bioinformatics is the new niche in biotechnology dealing with the application of software tools to biological data.

It is the symbiotic relationship between computational and biological sciences. While software engineers do not understand genes and genomes, biologists fail to comprehend programming concepts—bioinformatics helps to bridge this gap.

In the last few decades, advances in molecular biology and the availability of the latest equipment for research in this field have allowed the increasingly rapid sequencing of large portions of the genomes of several species. This inundation of data drove both biologists and software engineers into the field of bioinformatics to analyse this varied data and to arrive at meaningful biological conclusions. Thus, we can say that the field of bioinformatics gained a real identity in the mid-1980s. Though still an emerging field, it is rapidly gaining importance. So much so that software engineers who once wrote algorithms for big multi-national companies, telecom industries and banks, are now writing algorithms for analysing the human genome.

Gene sequences, which are of great interest and importance to the biologists, are simply codes that direct the production of proteins which in turn regulate all life's processes including the state of health. Both genome and proteome sequences help to understand many life's processes better. It also helps to understand the genetic make-up of people, which knowledge can be applied in human healthcare systems. But sequencing is a Herculian task—given the genome sequence of any organism, biologists find it difficult to recognise start codons, stop codons, promoter sequences, introns (non-coding sequences), exons (coding sequences) and also transcription factors (factors that initiate the synthesis of proteins from DNA sequences).

It is here that software engineers have helped and can continue to help the biologists—they can write computer programs that accurately predict the sequences. Genome-scale sequencing projects have led to an explosion of genetic sequences available for automated analysis. Popular sequence databases, such as GenBank and EMBL, have been growing at an exponential rate. This deluge of information has necessitated the careful storage, cataloguing and indexing of genetic data.

The benefits of bioinformatics to society therefore lie in harnessing the information pertaining to genetic functions and the functions of proteins and correlating them to the health conditions of people. Reduced to practical targets, the most pressing tasks in bioinformatics involve the analysis of sequences. This analysis involves:

- Finding the genes in the DNA sequences of various organisms
- Developing methods to predict the structure and/or function of newly discovered proteins and structural RNA sequences
- Clustering protein sequences into families of related sequences and the development of protein models
- Aligning similar proteins and generating phylogenetic trees to examine evolutionary relationships

The concepts given below emerged as the core ideas behind bioinformatics.

1. Data representation
2. Concept of similarity

DATA REPRESENTATION

DNA is coated with proteins that bind to specific sequences. This helps to untwist the helix to allow gene expression or wind it up into tightly packed super coils. Far from being a static archive of blueprints, DNA is a complex, dynamic, three-dimensional molecule. And yet we are able to represent all of this as a simple string of the characters A, C, G and T—bioinformatics help us to do so.

CONCEPT OF SIMILARITY

Evolution has operated on every sequence that we see today. It conserves genes that encode important proteins and the sequences that are involved in gene regulation. Sequences that encode useful functions are transferred, like code modules, from one organism to another.

It is possible to predict the three-dimensional structure of a protein using software tools that have been derived from our knowledge of mathematics, physics, chemistry and most importantly, from the X-ray crystal structure analysis of other proteins with similar amino acid sequences. This is the perfect input for computer analysis. Without it, it would have been impossible to even envision a project on the scale of the Human Genome Project. Algorithms for comparing sequences and finding similar regions are at the heart of bioinformatics. At many different levels, these algorithms are used to find genes, determine their functions, study their regulation and assess how they, and entire genomes, have evolved over time.

The evolution of bioinformatics can be divided into three stages. The subject, as of today, has evolved to the level between the first and second stages. The third stage is a prediction of where bioinformatics will be in a few years. Each stage has its own core issues to deal with. The stages have been briefly described below.

STAGE 1: The earliest and simplest task of bioinformatics is the creation and maintenance of databases of nucleic acids and protein sequences. With the advances in molecular biology techniques, efficiency of sequencing has improved dramatically. As storage of sequence information is no more a complex task, bioinformatics has moved on to its next phase.

STAGE 2: Fully sequencing a human genome is undoubtedly a great achievement, but it is by no means the final destination of modern biomedicine. In this phase, bioinformatics will be focussing on data mining within sequence databases. The first task will be finding the genes and their functions in the genome. Then, the functions and structures of the protein products of these genes will have to be predicted and classified. Finally, a biological molecular network will be outlined, and interactions of genes and proteins in this network made clear.

STAGE 3: Subsequently, individual genomic profiles will be used in pharmacology, disease treatment and prevention. The quality of medical care will be significantly improved in this phase, and bioinformatics will substantially affect the healthcare scenario.

Thus, through all its stages, bioinformatics offers an exciting array of opportunities to biologists and entrepreneurs to discover how living systems operate, metabolise and maintain their health.

Chapter 1

Basic Terminology

This chapter starts with the steps involved in running a C program. As this will necessarily require what is known as a compiler, an introduction to the compiler environment, Turbo C (TC), used for C programming is also given. Without getting into the nitty-gritty details of creating a program, we then try out a sample program with TC. After this brief look into the practical computer world, an introduction to various basic data types and other basic terminology in C is given. The chapter ends by jump starting into computational biology with simple programs.

Steps in Executing a C Program

Step 1: Use Turbo C editor to create a source file with your source code[1]
Step 2: Compile the source code to create an object file
Step 3: Link the compiled code to create an executable file
Step 4: Run or execute the program to verify its output

Step 1

Turbo C has a built-in editor. We can view the commands available on the menu bar of the computer monitor. Please consult the Turbo C manual or online help for more details on editor commands. In case of any problems with the built-in editor, it is possible to use more common editors like Notepad, edit in MSDOS, Word, and Word Perfect in ASCII

1 A source code is a sequence of statements written in a computer language, but which is not yet executable.

mode etc to create a program file. Note that all C program source files have a `.c` file extension.

STEP 2

Before your C program can be run on a computer, it must be translated from source code to what is known as an object code. This translation is performed by a program called a *compiler*. The compiler generates a disc file containing the *object code* from the source program.

To compile 'bio.c' (the sample program given in this chapter) from DOS shell (wherein the computer executes your commands after a prompt as opposed to clicking on icons), use the command given below

```
tcc bio.c
```

The other option is to use the built-in Compile menu item/icon from Turbo C (consult online help or manual for more information)

After compilation, the object file name is the same as the source file but instead of the `.c` extension, it has an `.OBJ` extension

STEP 3

The object file has to be then connected to a function library in order to run the functions that are being referred to in the source code, like `printf`, `scanf` etc. This process is called *linking* and it is performed by a program called a *linker*.

To link a file to Turbo C's function library use the following DOS command prompt

```
> tcc -l bio.obj
```

The other option is to use the Link menu item/icon to link your program to Turbo C IDE (interactive development environment). `bio.obj` is, of course, the name of our sample program.

Linking creates an executable file with an `.EXE` extension that is ready to run.

STEP 4

Run the program by entering its name from the command prompt or by pressing ALT-F5 from IDE to test whether the program functions properly.

If after executing the program, the results are different from what you expected or there is an error in the program, you need to go back to STEP 1. Identify the problem and correct the source code. When you make a change to the source code, you will need to re-compile and re-link the program to create a corrected version of the executable file.

RUNNING A SIMPLE PROGRAM: AN EXAMPLE

Let us try the four steps in executing a program which we learnt in the previous section with `bio.c`. This program basically prints a welcome message to bioinformatics students. Make sure that you have understood how to use the TURBO C editor and compiler before starting.

To store all the programs that you might try while reading this text, create a working directory in C:\Example.

STEP 1: ENTER THE PROGRAM IN TURBO EDITOR USING THE KEYBOARD

```
1: #include <stdio.h>
2: main()
3: {
4: printf("Welcome to Bioinformatics\n")
5: return 0;
6: }
```

Save the program under the file name `bio.c` by pressing ALT+F+S.

STEP 2: COMPILE BIO.C PROGRAM USING TURBO C COMPILER

Compile `bio.c` by pressing ALT+F9 in Turbo IDE or by using the command

```
tcc bio.c
```

from the command prompt. The compiler will display the error message given below.

```
bio.c (5): Error: ';' expected
```

This message obviously indicates that a semicolon is expected at line number 5 of the program. However, if you notice, there is already a semicolon present at the end of the instruction at line number 5. If you are still more observant, you will notice that there is no semicolon in line number 4—though the error is at line number 4, the compiler reports the error at line number 5. The reason for this is that the compiler can only understand the errors in a previous instruction after encountering the next instruction, which in this case is line number 5.

Place a semicolon at the end of line 4 and re-compile the program. Please note that by correcting one compilation error in multiple errors, all other errors can be fixed. Try to delete the quotation marks in the `printf` statement and find out for yourself.

STEP 3: LINK THE BIO.C PROGRAM

Press F9 to link your program or type

```
tcc -l bio.obj
```

to create `bio.exe`.

Errors might occur at this stage due to spelling mistakes of the functions referred to in the standard libraries. Please verify the function spellings and the presence of such libraries in case of link errors.

STEP 4: RUN THE PROGRAM

Press CTRL+F9 to execute `bio.exe`.

KEYWORDS IN C LANGUAGE

All computer languages have terms, called identifiers, which are used to name entities like integers, characters etc. An *identifier* in C consists of a sequence of letters (upper or lower case), digits or underscored characters. All such identifiers that are reserved by C language for only one special purpose are called *keywords*. A keyword has to be used only for the purpose it is meant for in the language and cannot be otherwise used in a program. Table 1.1 list the keywords in C.

Table 1.1 Reserved identifiers

auto	break	case	char	continue	default
do	double	else	enum	extern	float
for	goto	if	int	long	
return	short	sizeof	static	struct	switch
typedef	union	unsigned	void	while	

VARIABLES AND VARIABLE DECLARATION

A *variable* is a data name that may be used to store data values. This means that when we use a variable name in a program we are referring to the data stored in that memory location. A variable name can be aptly chosen by the programmer to reflect its function or nature in the program. Some examples of such names are `DNA`, `protein`, `pH` and `enzyme`.

A variable can be declared to be of a particular basic data type using the format

```
data type <variable name> = initial value
```

EXAMPLE: `char dna = 'a';`

As illustrated in Fig. 1.1, what the above declaration does is to name a location in the computer's memory as 'dna' and assign the value 'a' to it.

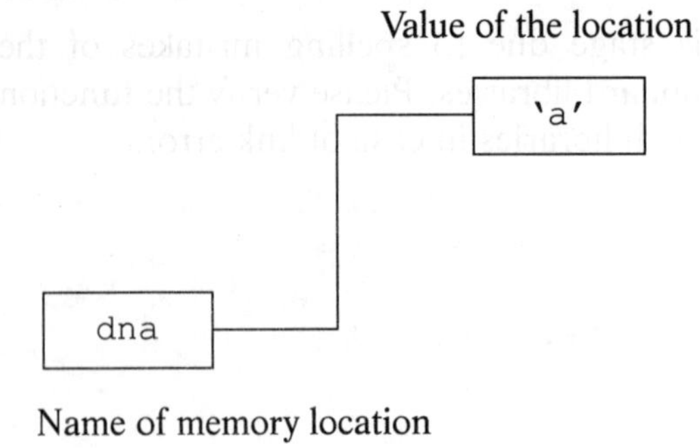

Fig. 1.1 Variable declaration

BASIC DATA TYPES

Table 1.2 briefly explains the basic data types in C programming. A variable can be defined using any of the basic types.

Table 1.2 Basic data types

Variable type	Keyword	Bytes	Range	Meaning
Character	`char`	1	–128 to 127	This type can take single character values
Integer	`int`	2	–32768 to 32767	This type can take integer values—values without any decimal point
Short integer	`short`	2	–32768 to 32767	This type can take in values which require less memory than `int` type but with reduced accuracy

(Continues...

... Continued)

Variable type	Keyword	Bytes	Range	Meaning
Long integer	`long`	4	–2,147,483,648 to 2,147,438,647	This type can take in values which require more memory than `int` type but with enhanced accuracy
Unsigned character	`unsigned char`	1	0 to255	Same as `char` but does not allow for sign extension
Unsigned integer	`unsigned int`	2	0 to 65535	This takes only positive integer values
Unsigned short integer	`unsigned short`	2	0 to 65535	
Unsigned long integer	`unsigned long`	4	0 to 4,294,967,295	
Single-precision	`float`	4		This takes floating point values that may contain decimal places
Double-precision	`double`	8		This takes floating point values with extended accuracy

We will explain the basic data type `char` and `int` in more detail as they are the most common types used in bioinformatics.

`char` This data type is used to store letters, digits, special characters and blanks. The syntax for declaring a character type variable is

```
char <variable type>
```

EXAMPLE: `char gene;`

`int` This data type is used to store numerical values (both positive and negative). There are four different categories of `int` as mentioned in Table 1.2—the long and short integer, and the unsigned long and short integer. The syntax for declaring `int` data type variable is as follows:

```
int <variable name>
```

EXAMPLE: `int chrom;`

CONSTANTS AND FORMAT SPECIFIERS

Unlike a variable, the value stored in a constant cannot be changed during the execution of a program. If we try to change the value of a constant, an error is generated either at the time of compiling or during execution. There are several kinds of constants. However, in this section we will only discuss the following constants.

1. Integer constant
2. Character constant
3. Symbolic constant

INTEGER CONSTANT

The *integer constant* can be of data type `int`, `unsigned int`, `long int` and `unsigned long int`.

Integer constants can be represented in three different number systems namely decimal (base 10), octal (base 8) or hexadecimal (base 16). In the decimal system, only 0 to 9 digits are used, whereas in the octal system 0 to 7 digits are used. The hexadecimal system uses 0 to 9 digits and letters from A to F.

EXAMPLE: `const int seq_lenth = 40;`

CHARACTER CONSTANT

A *character constant* is a sequence of one or more characters enclosed in single quotes as in 'x'. A term often interlinked with a character constant is the escape sequence. An *escape sequence* changes the meaning of a normal character, making it a constant. The following escape sequences can be used to represent character constants.

horizontal tab	HT	\t
vertical tab	VT	\v
backspace	BS	\b
carriage return	CR	\r
form feed	FF	\f
audible alert	BEL	\a
octal number	ooo	\<octal value>
hex number	hh	\<hex value>

A common example of using backslash in defining a character constant is \0, which specifies the character NUL.

SYMBOLIC CONSTANT

A *symbolic constant* is nothing but a symbol in a given program. The value of the symbolic constant, as any constant, cannot be changed. It is defined only once and used as and when there is a need in the program, by using the symbol name. The compiler will replace any occurrence of the symbol in the program by its value.

A symbolic constant can be defined by using `#define` directive or a constant keyword.

EXAMPLE: `#define MATCH 1`

This symbol is used often in bioinformatics to match scores during sequence analysis. The match value can be any number as per the requirement but should be defined only once. If any change is required to be made, we have to return to the `define` directive.

FORMAT SPECIFIERS

Format specifiers are used to output/input the values stored by basic data types on the display media or to memory. Table 1.3 explains the various formats that can be used with basic data types.

Table 1.3 Format specifiers

Data type	Format specifier
`char`	%c
`short int`	%d
`int or signed int`	%d
`unsigned int`	%u
`long int`	%ld
`float`	%f
`double`	%lf

EXAMPLE: The following program will illustrate the use of format specifiers.

PROGRAM 1.1: BIOFORM.C

```
/*
Program name: bioform.c
Description: To display the chromo number and purine
nucleosides
*/
```

```
#include <stdio.h>
main()
{
  int CHROM = 5;
  char nucleoside = 'A';
  printf("Number of human CHROM\n");
  printf("Purine nucleoside\n");

  printf("Number of human CHROM: %d\n", CHROM);
  printf("Purine nucleoside: %c\n", nucleoside);
  return;
}
```

As you can see from the program, no matter what kind of integer `CHROM` is, when it is displayed the format specifier %d changes its format to a `short int`. Let us see the output of the program.

OUTPUT

```
Number of human CHROM
Purine nucleoside
Number of human CHROM: 5
Purine nucleoside: A
```

OTHER BASIC TERMINOLOGY

Before we proceed further, it might be better to familiarise ourselves with other terms which are often used while creating a program, like main function and arguments.

MAIN FUNCTION

The term *`main`* is used in C programming to indicate the beginning of the program execution. The `main` routine may have arguments (explained in the next section) that are placed in between open and close parentheses next to the term '`main`'. Even if it does not have arguments, the `main` routine has open and close braces. All program statements are placed in between these braces for execution. The program execution begins at the open brace and ends at the closing brace. The closing brace of the `main` is the logical end of the program. Looking at PROGRAM 1.1 in the previous section, we can understand the structure of the `main` routine.

PROGRAM 1.1 has no arguments. You will also notice that every program statement in a C program is terminated by a semicolon. The '*printf*' statement helps to see the output on the display.

COMMAND LINE ARGUMENTS

When a C program is called (made use of by another program), the arguments on the command line are made available using an argument count, *argc* and a pointer[2], *argv*, to an array of character strings containing the arguments. The two arguments `argc` and `argv` are placed in between open and close parentheses next to the term '`main`'. The following simple program illustrates the command line argument. The arguments are passed at the command prompt by typing

```
<program name> Space <argument1>
```

This program prints only the first argument. However, it can be modified to print all the arguments passed to the program at the command prompt.

PROGRAM 1.2: CMDLINE.C

```
#include <stdio.h>
main(argc,argv)
int argc;
char *argv[];
{
  if(argc <2)
  {
      printf("Usage: cmdline <argument>\n");
      exit(0);
  }
  printf("\nCommand Line Argument is %s\n",argv[1]);
}
```

OUTPUT

```
> cmdline

Usage: cmdline <argument>

cmdline 10

Command Line Argument is 10

cmdline bio

Command Line Argument is bio
```

---

[2] Please refer to Chapter 7 to understand more about pointers

DISCUSSION

In the above program, if `argc` (argument count) is less than 2, it would be terminated i.e. if argc is equal to 1 then there is no command line arguments except the program name. If argc is 2 then,

`argv[0]` points to `cmdline`
`argv[1]` points to `bio`

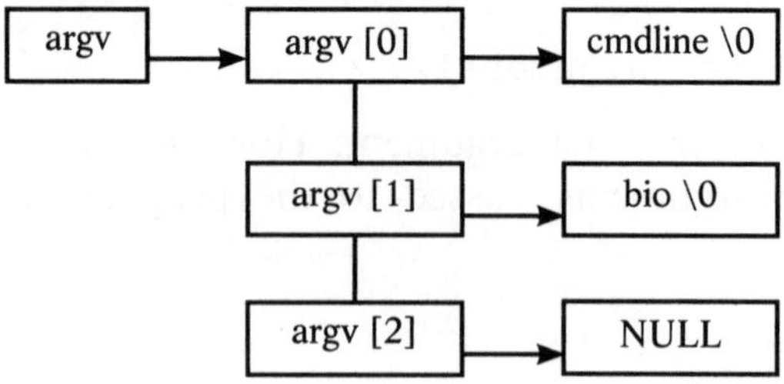

`argv[argc]` is always null and each argument is terminated by a null character.

LOCAL VARIABLE

We have already discussed variables, but there is another type of variable, different only because of its usage, called the local variable. *Local* or *automatic variables* are declared inside a function in which they will be utilised. This means that they are created when a function is called and destroyed automatically when we exit the function. Local variables are private to the function in which they are declared and therefore are also referred to as *internal variables*.

PROGRAM 1.3: DNA_VARIABLES.C

```
main()
{
  /* nucleosides are 'a', 't','g','c' */
  char nucleoside;
  nucleoside = 'a';
  printf("Nucleoside in DNA is %c\n", nucleoside);
}
```

In this program variable '`nucleoside`' is a local or automatic variable.

HEADER FILES

Header files are a central repository of information like definitions and declarations that can be shared by many programs. For example, PROGRAM 1.1 includes `stdio.h` header in its program. Therefore, all the definitions and declarations of header `stdio` are available to PROGRAM 1.1.

As we can see in PROGRAM 1.1, header files are included in a program using `#include` directive. They can be included in one of the following ways

1. #include <file name>
2. #include "file name"

COMMENTS

Comments are non-executable program statements. They are used only for documentation purposes and to bring more clarity to the program flow which would help during the maintenance of programs and correcting errors. In C, anything in between /* and */ is treated as a comment.

Chapter 2

Operators

An operator is a symbol in C that performs an operation, an activity or an action. They are used in programs to manipulate data and variables and usually form a part of a mathematical or logical expression. The language C supports a rich set of operators. They fall into the following categories.

1. Assignment operators
2. Arithmetic operators
3. Increment and decrement operators
4. Relational operators
5. Logical operators
6. Ternary operators
7. Bitwise operators
8. Special operators

Assignment Operators

There are several assignment operators. They are

```
=       *=
/=      %=
+=      -=
<<=     >>=
&=      ^=
|=
```

An assignment expression has a left operand, an operator and a value. The association of operators is from right to left, unlike how we usually read a text. The operator '=' assigns the value or the result of an expression to the variable or, what we call here, the left operand. The value or result is stored in the left operand after the assignment has taken place.

```
<variable name> = value;
```

EXAMPLE: `aa = 10;`

Assignment operations for amino acids (aa) along with the statements are listed in Table 2.1.

Table 2.1 Usage of assignment operators

Statement	Modified statement
`aa = aa+1`	`aa+ = 1`
`aa = aa-1`	`aa- = 1`
`aa = aa*(n+1)`	`aa* = n+1`
`aa = aa/(n+1)`	`aa/ = n+1`

ARITHMETIC OPERATORS

The basic arithmetic operators are listed in Table 2.2.

Table 2.2 Arithmetic operators

Operator	Description	Example
+	Addition or unary plus	`mrna + trna`
–	Subtraction or unary minus	`mrna - trna`
*	Multiplication	`aa1 * aa2`
/	Division	`a/t`
%	Gives the remainder when the first operand is divided by the second operand	–

The binary + and – operators have the same precedence[1], which is lower than the precedence of *, / and %, which is in turn lower than the unary + and –. This means that when there is an expression containing all these operators, the compiler calculates the unary + and – first, the *, / and % next, and the binary + and – operators last. Arithmetic operators associate left to right.

[1] Operator precedence describes the order in which C reads expressions.

INCREMENT AND DECREMENT OPERATORS

The C language also has increment and decrement operators (Table 2.3). The increment operator ++ adds 1 to its operand, while the decrement operator -- subtracts 1.

Table 2.3 Increment and decrement mathematical operators

Operator	Description	Example
++	Increments the operand by one	`++pH, pH++`
--	Decrements the operand by one	`--pH, pH--`

These operators cannot be applied to constants; they can only be used on variables.

`++pH` or `pH++` is equivalent to `pH = pH+1`
`--pH` or `pH--` is equivalent to `pH = pH-1`

There is a slight difference between `++pH` and `pH++`. The term `++pH` refers to an operation in which `pH` has been incremented by 1 and this value is assigned to the variable `pH`. While the term `pH++` refers to an operation in which the `pH` value is used and then incremented by 1.

The program given below illustrates the use of the increment operator.

PROGRAM 2.1: BUFFER_PH.C

```
#include <stdio.h>
main()
{
/* This program demonstrates how to increase or
decrease the pH value of a buffer */

int weak_buffer = 7, strong_buffer;
printf("\n pH value of weak buffer before
incrementing is %d\n", weak_buffer);
weak_buffer++;
printf("\n pH value of weak buffer after
incrementing is %d\n", weak_buffer);

/*
First take the value of the weak buffer into the
strong buffer and then increase the value of the
weak buffer by one i.e. to say, post increment of
weak buffer
```

```
*/
strong_buffer = weak_buffer++;
printf("\n pH value of strong buffer with assignment
of weak buffer is %d\n", strong_buffer);
printf("\n pH value of weak buffer with post
increment is %d\n", weak_buffer);

/*
First increase the value of the weak buffer by one
and then take the value of the weak buffer into the
strong buffer i.e. to say  pre increment of weak
buffer
*/

strong_buffer = ++weak_buffer;
printf("\n pH value of strong buffer with assignment
of weak buffer is %d\n", strong_buffer);
printf("\n pH value of weak buffer with pre
increment is %d\n", weak_buffer);
}
```

OUTPUT

```
pH value of weak buffer before incrementing is 7

pH value of weak buffer after incrementing is 8

pH value of strong buffer with assignment of weak
buffer is 8

pH value of weak buffer with post increment is 9

pH value of strong buffer with assignment of weak
buffer is 10

pH value of weak buffer with pre increment is 10
```

RELATIONAL OPERATORS

Relational operators are used to compare two entities in order to make decisions after the comparison. There are four relational operators, < (lesser), > (greater), <= (lesser or equal) and >= (greater or equal). A relational operator yields 0 if the specified relation is false and 1 if it is true i.e. the value of a relational expression is either one or zero. The relational operators <, >=, <, and <= all have the same precedence and follow in precedence the equality operators = and !=. This whole class of operators has a lower precedence than arithmetic operators.

EXAMPLE: `10 < 20 is true whereas 20 < 10 is false`

LOGICAL OPERATORS

The language C supports three logical operators—AND, OR and NOT. Table 2.4 lists the logical operators. The two operators && and || are used to test more than one condition and make a decision based on the evaluation. Logical operators are evaluated from left to right.

Table 2.4 Logical operators

Operator	Description	Example
&&	AND	`Donor && Acceptor`
||	OR	`Donor || Acceptor`
!	NOT	`!Donor`

In the example given in Table 2.4, the expression `Donor && Acceptor` is evaluated as True or False. This is the way logical operators deal with all expressions.

The truth table[2] for logical operators `&&` and `||` is given in Table 2.5.

Table 2.5 Truth table (T: True; F: False)

Donor	Acceptor	Donor & Acceptor	Donor || Acceptor
T	T	T	T
T	F	F	T
F	T	F	T
F	F	F	F

TERNARY OPERATOR

A ternary operator is one which takes three arguments. The ternary operator in C is `'?:'`. With this operator, we can construct conditional expressions of the form

```
exp1 ? exp2 : exp3
```

where `exp1`, `exp2` and `exp3` are expressions.

---

[2] A truth table is a mathematical table which computes all the possible values of an expression, given the values of its components.

Here, `exp1` is evaluated first. If `exp1` is true i.e. the condition in `exp1` is satisfied, `exp2` is evaluated and its value becomes the value of the expression. If `exp1` is false, `exp3` is evaluated and its value becomes the value of the expression.

The program given below uses the ternary operator to determine the gene length based on exon length or intron length.

PROGRAM 2.2: GENLEN.C

```
#include <stdio.h>
main()
{
  /* This program demonstrates the true or false
conditional branch based on the ternary operator's
expression or statement (?)  */

int exon_length = 10, intron_length = 15, gene;
gene = (exon_length > intron_length) ? exon_length:
intron_length;

printf("\n Exon length  is %d\n", exon_length);
printf("\n Intron length  is %d\n", intron_length);
printf("\n Intron gene length is %d\n", gene);
}
```

OUTPUT

```
Exon length is 10
Intron length is 15
Intron gene length is 15
```

OPERATOR PRECEDENCE

Table 2.6 lists all the C operators in the order of decreasing precedence. All operators at the same level that are grouped together have the same precedence and therefore all operators in the same level get executed by association. Operators higher in the table have a higher precedence. The "Association" column on the right indicates the evaluation order.

Table 2.6 Operator precedence

<table>
<tr><th>Operator</th><th>Description</th><th>Association</th><th>Level</th></tr>
<tr><td>()</td><td>Function call</td><td>Left to right</td><td>1</td></tr>
<tr><td>[]</td><td>Array element reference</td><td></td><td></td></tr>
<tr><td>-></td><td>Pointer to structure member reference</td><td></td><td></td></tr>
<tr><td>.</td><td>Structure member reference</td><td></td><td></td></tr>
<tr><td>!</td><td>Logical negation</td><td>Right to left</td><td>2</td></tr>
<tr><td>~</td><td>One's complement</td><td></td><td></td></tr>
<tr><td>++</td><td>Increment</td><td></td><td></td></tr>
<tr><td>- -</td><td>Decrement</td><td></td><td></td></tr>
<tr><td>* (in direction)</td><td>Pointer reference</td><td></td><td></td></tr>
<tr><td>&</td><td>Address</td><td></td><td></td></tr>
<tr><td>sizeof</td><td>Size of an object</td><td></td><td></td></tr>
<tr><td>*</td><td>Multiplication</td><td>Left to right</td><td>3</td></tr>
<tr><td>/</td><td>Division</td><td></td><td></td></tr>
<tr><td>%</td><td>Modulus</td><td></td><td></td></tr>
<tr><td>+</td><td>Addition</td><td>Left to right</td><td>4</td></tr>
<tr><td>-</td><td>Subtraction</td><td></td><td></td></tr>
<tr><td><<</td><td>Left shift</td><td>Left to right</td><td>5</td></tr>
<tr><td>>></td><td>Right shift</td><td></td><td></td></tr>
<tr><td><</td><td>Less than</td><td>Left to right</td><td>6</td></tr>
<tr><td><=</td><td>Less than or equal to</td><td></td><td></td></tr>
<tr><td>></td><td>Greater than</td><td></td><td></td></tr>
<tr><td>>=</td><td>Greater than or equal to</td><td></td><td></td></tr>
<tr><td>==</td><td>Equal</td><td>Left to right</td><td>7</td></tr>
<tr><td>!=</td><td>Not Equal</td><td></td><td></td></tr>
<tr><td>&</td><td>Bitwise AND</td><td>Left to right</td><td>8</td></tr>
<tr><td>^</td><td>Bitwise XOR</td><td>Left to right</td><td>9</td></tr>
<tr><td>|</td><td>Bitwise OR</td><td>Left to right</td><td>10</td></tr>
<tr><td>&&</td><td>Logical AND</td><td>Left to right</td><td>11</td></tr>
<tr><td>||</td><td>Logical OR</td><td>Left to right</td><td>12</td></tr>
<tr><td>?:</td><td>Conditional expression</td><td>Left to right</td><td>13</td></tr>
<tr><td>= += -= *= /= %= &= ^= |= <<= >>=</td><td>Assignment operators</td><td>Right to left</td><td>14</td></tr>
<tr><td>,</td><td>Comma separator</td><td>Right to left</td><td>15</td></tr>
</table>

Chapter 3

Statements and Control Flow

A control flow deals with the way or order in which computations are performed. In a C program, the statements get executed from top to bottom. Control statements help change the order of execution. Sometimes a change in program flow causes certain portions of the program to get executed a few or even multiple times. The control statement reduces the `GOTO` loop nature of the program and makes it more structured.

Conditional Statements

A program statement is a valid expression that is immediately followed by a semicolon. An expression such as

```
int exon_length = 10
```

becomes a statement if it is terminated by a semicolon. A group of statements that are declared within { } braces are called *statement blocks* or *compound statements*. In order to make execution of commands easier and faster, a block is treated as a single statement.

Example

```
{
  printf( "Welcome to    ");
  printf( "BioProgramming\n");
}
```

Conditional statements are expressions which are used to perform a sequence of steps depending on whether a pre-specified condition is satisfied or not. There are two kinds of conditional statements.

1. *`If-else`* statement
2. *`Switch`* statement

IF–ELSE STATEMENT

The *`if`* or *`if-else`* statement is used to make or express a decision between two or more courses of action. The format for a simple `if-else` statement is as given below.

```
if (expression)
  statement A or block of statements
else
  statement B or block of statements
```

Figure 3.1 briefly explains the `if-else` and the more intricate nested `if-else if-else` flow of statements.

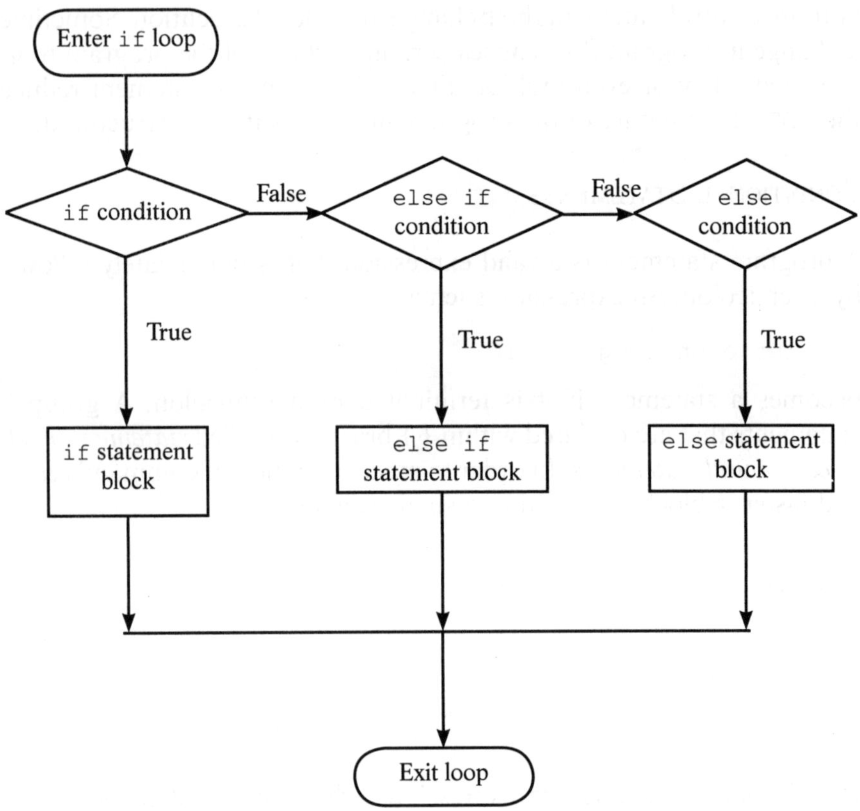

Fig. 3.1 The `if-else` control flow

Depending on the complexity of the conditions to be tested, the statements can be categorised as

1. Simple `if` statement
2. `If-else` statement
3. Nested `if . . . else` statement
4. `Else-if` ladder

Simple `If` Statement The program given below uses a simple `if` conditional expression to compare nucleosides and determine the number of purines and pyramidines.

PROGRAM 3.1: NONCLS.C

```
/* To determine the number of nucleosides */

#include <stdio.h>
main()
{
  /* define nucleosides */
  int a,t,g,c;
  int purines, pyramidines;
  printf("\n Enter respective values for nucleosides
<a,t,g,c> \n");
  scanf("%d%d%d%d", &a, &t,&g,&c);

  /* Compare the number of purines and pyramidines*/
  if (a - t == 0)
  {
     purines = a + g;
     pyramidines = t + c;
     printf("\n No of purines = %d\n", purines);
     printf("\n No of pyramidines=%d\n",
pyramidines);
  }
else printf("\n a and t should have same values\n");
}
```

OUTPUT

```
RUN 1
For a, t, g and c values of 10, 20, 30 and 40
respectively, the output is:

Enter respective values for nucleosides <a,t,g,c>
10
```

```
20
30
40
a and t should have same values
```

RUN 2

```
For a, t, g and c values of 10, 10, 20 and 30
respectively, the output is:

Enter respective values for nucleosides <a,t,g,c>
10
10
20
30

No of purines = 30
No of pyramidines = 40
```

If–Else Statement The program given below uses the `if-else` statement to compare two peptides and decide which of them is a polypeptide or a small peptide.

PROGRAM 3.2: PEPTIDE.C

```
/*
Description: Compares two peptides and determines
the type of the peptide i.e small or poly based on
the values inputted for the peptide. Let us assume
that the amino acid range for small peptide is <1-8>
whereas it is <9-50> for  a poly peptide

Assume peptide1 and peptide2 correspond to a small
and poly peptide respectively
*/

#include <stdio.h>
main()
{

/* Shows the type of the peptide */

int peptide1, peptide2;

printf("\nEnter the length for peptides < Small
Pept,Poly Pept >\n");
scanf("%d%d", &peptide1, &peptide2);
```

```
if (peptide1 < peptide2)
    {
        if (peptide1 < 8)
            {
        if( peptide2 > 8)
              printf("\n Entered 'aa' are both small
and poly peptides\n");
        else printf("\n Entered 'aa' are small
peptides\n");
            }
  else printf("\n Entered 'aa' are poly peptides\
n");
    }

else {
  if ( peptide2 > 8)
    {
     printf("\n Entered 'aa' are poly peptides\n");
    }
  else printf("\n Entered 'aa' are both small and
poly peptides\n");
    }
}
```

OUTPUT

```
C:\bio>peptide
Enter the length for peptides <Small Pept,Poly Pept>
2 6

Entered 'aa' are small peptides

C:\bio>peptide
Enter the length for peptides <Small Pept,Poly Pept>
9 12

Entered 'aa' are poly peptides

C:\bio>peptide
Enter the length for peptides <Small Pept,Poly Pept>
6 9

Entered 'aa' are both small and poly peptides

C:\bio>peptide
Enter the length for peptides <Small Pept,Poly Pept>
9 6

Entered 'aa' are both small and poly peptides
```

Nested If . . . Else Statement The `if-else` statement is generally used to make choices between two possible alternatives. If a choice is to be made between more than two possibilities, a nested `if-else` statement is used. Here, in the primary `if-else` statement block, the statement following the '`else`' is itself an `if-else` statement. Figure 3.2 shows the flow structure of a nested `if-else` statement to decide if a reaction can take place or not depending on temperature, change in enthalpy and entropy.

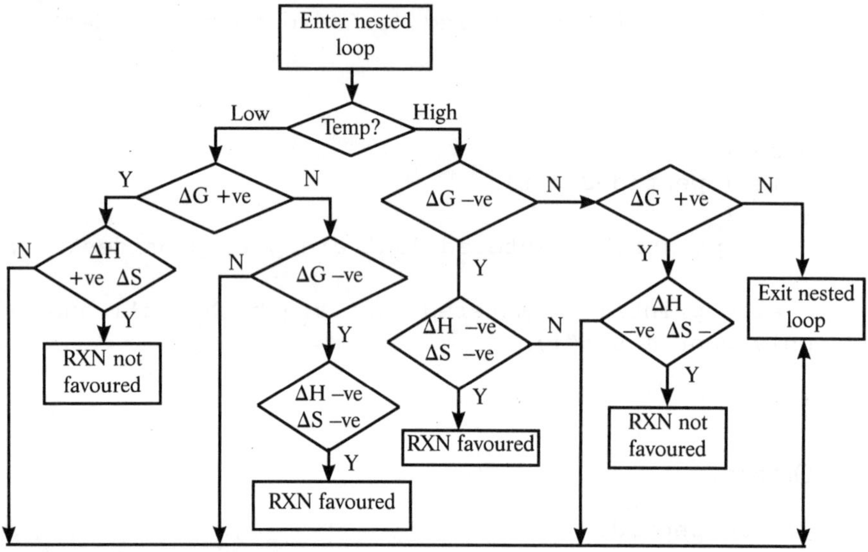

ΔG: change in free energy; ΔH: change in enthalpy; ΔS: change in entropy; T: temperature; RXN: reaction

Fig. 3.2 Nested conditional structure

It is obvious from the figure that too many `if` loops have been nested. Such a nested structure leads to lack of clarity. In such a case it is better to decompose the structure into small individual tasks i.e. functions, and then link all of them together.

PROGRAM 3.3 uses nested `if` blocks to determine which among three values has the maximum value. This program can be used while aligning amino acid sequences—using it recursively in a dynamic programming[1] matrix, we can find the maximal score value among diagonal, left and above cell scores.

---

[1] Dynamic programming, as you may know, is the process of finding an optimal solution to a problem by taking the optimal solution of its parts.

PROGRAM 3.3: MAXSCORE.C

```
#include <stdio.h>
main ()
{
int diagonal, left, above;
printf("Enter alignment scores for three sequences\
n");
scanf("%d %d %d", &diagonal ,&left , &above);

if(diagonal > left)
{
  if(diagonal > above)
     printf("\n %d is the max value\n", diagonal);
  else
     printf("\n %d is the max value\n", above);
}
else
{
  if(left> above)
        printf("\n %d is the max value\n", left);
  else
        printf("\n %d is the max value\n", above);
}
}
```

OUTPUT

```
Enter alignment scores for three sequences
6
90
78
90 is the max value
```

Else–If Ladder The `else-if` ladder statement is based upon nested `ifs`. The format is as follows:

```
if (expression)
  statement A or block of statements
  else if (expression)
        statement B or block of statements
        else if (expression)
  statement B or block of statements
```

The expressions are evaluated from the top downward. As soon as a condition is satisfied, the statement associated with it is executed, and the rest of the ladder is bypassed. The program given below uses the `else-if` *ladder* to decipher amino acids from codons and print the amino acid.

PROGRAM 3.4: DECIPHER.C

```
/* Deciphering amino acids from codon and printing the
amino acid. The nucleosides are a or u or g. Print the
codon only if glycine equals g,phenylalanine equals
'u' and lysine equals 'a' */

#include <stdio.h>
main()
{
char choice= '\0';
        printf("\nEnter base for glycine <g>\n");
scanf("%c", &choice);

if ( choice == 'g')  printf("\n The codon for
glycine is 'ggg'\n");
else
   {
    /* choice= '\0'; */
    printf("\nEnter base for phenylalanine <u>\n");
    fflush(stdin); /* This is required to invoke
scanf again */
    scanf("%c", &choice);
    if (choice == 'u') printf("\n The codon for
phenylalanine is 'uuu'\n");
       else
       {
         printf("\nEnter base for lysine <a> \n");
         fflush(stdin); /* Required call to invoke
scanf again*/
         scanf("%c", &choice);
   if (choice == 'a') printf("\n The codon for
lysine is 'aaa'\n");
       }
  }
}
```

OUTPUT

RUN 1

```
Enter base for glycine <g>
a
```

```
Enter base for phenylalanine <u>
u
the codon for phenylalanine is 'uuu'
```

RUN 2

```
Enter base for Glycine <g>
a

Enter base for phenylalanine <u>
a

Enter base for lysine <a>
a
The codon for lysine is 'aaa'
```

SWITCH

The `if` control statement works well when decisions are to be made from few alternatives. However, if there are too many alternatives to select from, the `if-else` structure is too tedious and confusing. In such cases the `switch` function is used. It works as a multi-way decision-making tool to test whether various alternatives satisfy the conditional expression.

The general format of a switch statement is as shown below.

```
switch(expression)
{
  case value 1:
  block 1
  break;
  case value 2:
  block 2
  break;
  …….
  …….
  …….

  default:
  default block;
}
statement X;
```

The expression specified in the `switch` is compared with case value 1, case value 2 and so on. If any of the conditions is satisfied then that particular block is executed. The `break` statement at the end of each block signals the end of the particular case and causes the program to exit from the `switch` statement. The control is then transferred to the statement X following the `switch`. The default statement is optional—if it is not present, and all case matches fail, no action takes place and control is transferred to the statement X.

Figure 3.3 briefly describes the `switch` flow.

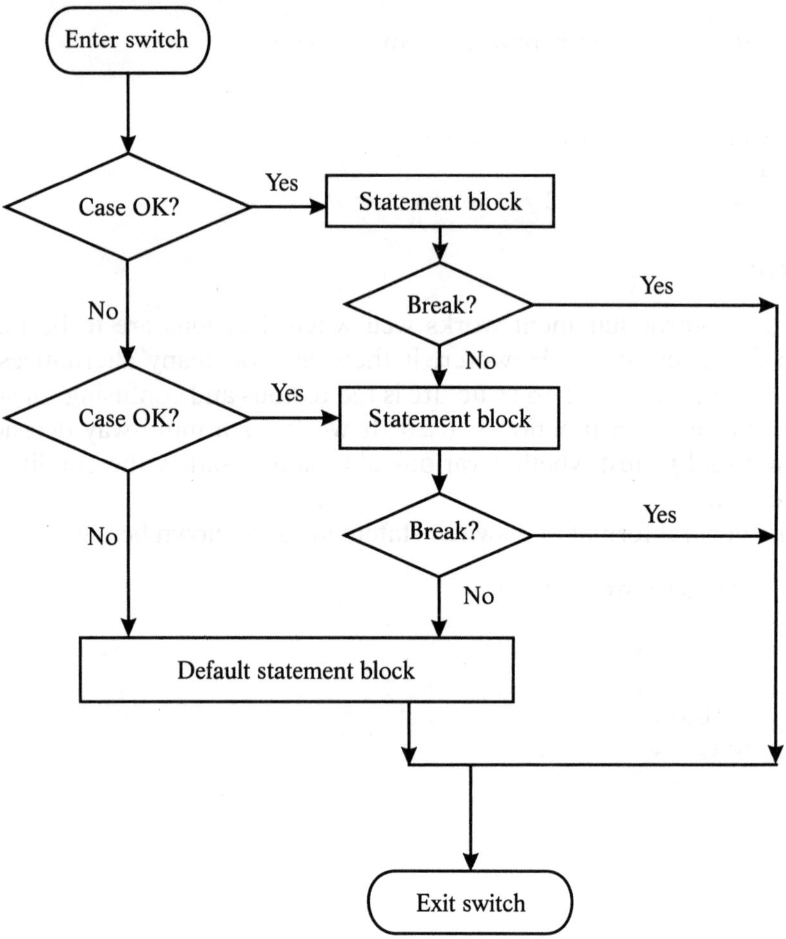

Fig. 3.3 `Switch` flow chart

The program given below determines the type of DNA depending on the base number.

PROGRAM 3.5: DNA_TYPES.C

```
#include <stdio.h>
main()
{
  int base_number;
  printf("\n Enter number of bases in DNA \n");
  scanf("%d", &base_number);

  switch (base_number)
  {
  case 10:
  printf("\n Type of DNA is B\n");
  break;

  case 11:
        printf("\n Type of DNA is A\n");
        break;

  case 12:
        printf("\n Type of DNA is Z\n");
        break;

  default:
        printf("\n No valid DNA type for this base
number\n");
        printf("\n Enter base <12 or 10 or 11> and
try again \n");
  break;
}
}
```

OUTPUT

```
Enter number of bases in DNA
a

No valid DNA type for this base number

Enter base <12 or 10 or 11> and try again

Enter number of bases in DNA
10

Type of DNA is B
```

ITERATIONS OR LOOPS

The conditional statements covered earlier in this chapter can only execute a statement or block of statements once based on the condition. However, in some situations, it may be required that the statements or block be executed more than once. The language C provides three different kinds of iteration or loop statements.

1. `for` statement
2. `while` statement
3. `do-while` statement

THE FOR STATEMENT

The *for* statement executes a statement or block statements for a certain number of times.
The general format of a `for` statement is as shown below.

```
for (initialisation, test condition, increment or
decrement)
{
  statement or block of statements
}
```

`for` loops are appropriate where the initialisation and increment or decrement are single statements and are logically related. We can also execute an infinite loop using the `for` statement. The format is as follows

```
for( ; ;)
{
  . . . . . .
  . . . . . .
}
```

The infinite loop can be broken by using the command `break` or `return`. The flow chart of `for` is given in Fig. 3.4.

The program given below prints a message multiple times

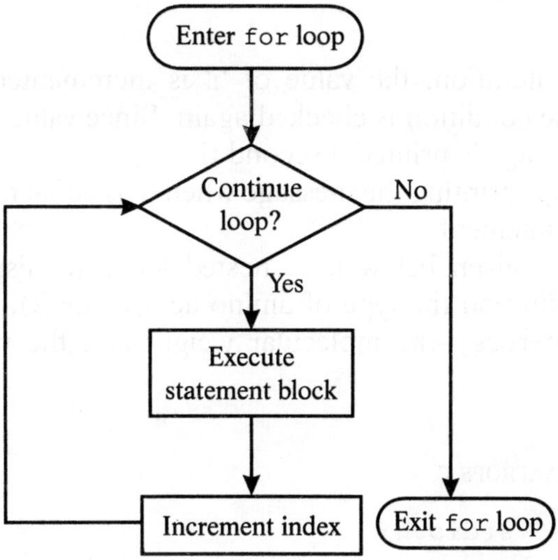

Fig. 3.4 The for flow chart

PROGRAM 3.6: PRINTMSG.C

```
#include <stdio.h>
main()
{
  int iteration;

  for ( iteration =1; iteration<=3; iteration++)
  {
        printf("\n amino acid Glycine\n");
  }
}
```

OUTPUT

```
amino acid Glycine

amino acid Glycine

amino acid Glycine
```

The for loop gets executed in the following manner.

STEP 1

The variable 'i' is initialised to 1 in the beginning. Then the test condition whether 'i < 3' is checked. In the first iteration, the message is printed as the value of 'i' is less than 3.

STEP 2

In the second iteration, the value of 'i' is incremented and its value becomes 2. The condition is checked again. Since value of 'i' is still less than 3, the message is printed a second time.

The loop stops printing the message when 'i' is equal to 3 and the loop exits the `for` statement.

The program given below uses nested loops to display the codon pattern depending on the type of amino acid (L or R). It also displays two basic properties—the molecular weight and the volume—of the amino acid.

PROGRAM 3.7: AAPROPS.C

```
#include <stdio.h>
main()
{
  int aa_acid,am_type, counter;
  char amino_acid;
  unsigned int para = 0;
  printf("Enter the number of amino acids <Less or
equal 3>\n");
  scanf("%d", &aa_acid);
        fflush(stdin);
  if(aa_acid > 3 ) { printf("Retry with <= 3 \n");
  exit(0); }

/* The outer for loop for each amino acid displays
the codon pattern depending on the type of amino
acid */

for (counter=1; counter < aa_acid; counter++)
{
  printf("\n Input amino acid in CAPS\n");
  scanf("%c", &amino_acid);
              fflush(stdin);

  if (amino_acid == 'L')
  {
        printf("\n Codon for amino acid %c is CUU,
CUC,CUA,CUG\n",amino_acid);

/* The inner loop displays two properties of the
amino acid-the molecular weight and volume when 1 is
pressed and volume when 0 is pressed*/
```

```
  for (am_type = 1; am_type < 3; am_type++)
        {
              printf("\n Enter 1 or 0 value\n");
              scanf("%u", &para);

              if(para) printf("\n Molecular weight
is 113.8 \n");
              printf("\n Volume is 124.0\n");

        }
        } /* end of if */

        if (amino_acid == 'R')
        {
        printf("\n Codon for amino acid %c is CGU,
CGC,CGA,CGG\n", amino_acid);

/* The inner loop displays two properties of the
amino acid—the molecular weight when 1 is pressed
and volume when 0 is pressed*/

  for (am_type = 1; am_type < 3; am_type++)
        {
        printf("\n Enter 1 or 0 value\n");
        scanf("%u", &para);

        if(para) printf("\n Molecular weight is
157.2 \n");
        printf("\n Volume is 148\n");
        }
        } /* end if */
      } /* End of outer for loop */
} /* End of the program */
```

OUTPUT

```
Enter the number of amino acids <Less or equal 3>
4
Retry with <= 3

C:\>aaprops
Enter the number of amino acids <Less or equal 3>
3

Enter amino acid < L or R>
L
```

```
Codon for amino acid L is CUU, CUC,CUA,CUG

Enter 1 or 0 value
1

Molecular weight is 113.8

Volume is 124.0

Enter 1 or 0 value
0

Volume is 124.0

Enter amino acid < L or R>
```

THE WHILE STATEMENT

The format of the *while* statement is given below.

```
while (test condition)
{
  statement block
}
```

No initialisation is required to execute the `while` statement. Therefore, it is a natural loop statement. The `while` command is an entry controlled loop statement. The test condition is usually a relation expression which gets evaluated as either true or false. If the condition is evaluated as true, the statement block is executed. At the end of each iteration, the test condition is evaluated and the loop continues to operate till the condition is evaluated as false. Then the control is transferred out of the loop.

The flow chart of the `while` iteration is given in Fig. 3.5.

The program given below prints all the even chromo numbers using the `while` iteration.

PROGRAM 3.8: EVNCHROM.C

```
#include <stdio.h>
main()
{

/* An illustration of the working of a while loop
using even chromosomes */

int chrom_number,even_chrom = 2;
printf("\n Enter  chrom number\n");
scanf("%d", &chrom_number);
```

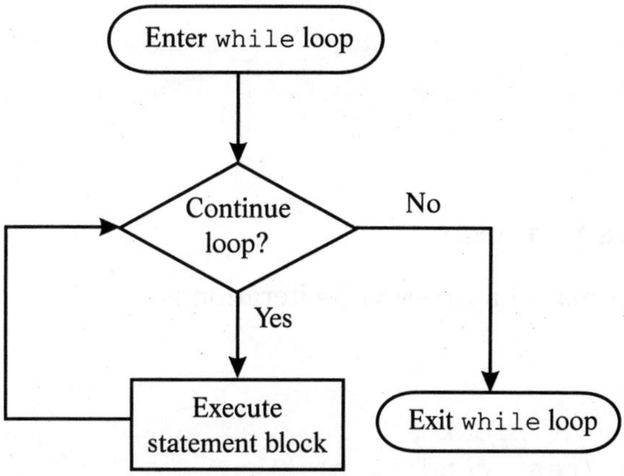

Fig. 3.5 The `while` flow chart

```
   if (chrom_number < 20 )
   {
         if (chrom_number > 1) printf("\n Even
 numbers of chromosomes are \n");
         else printf("Enter chrom number > 1 for even
 chromosomes\n");
         while ( even_chrom <= chrom_number)
         {
               printf("\n %d\n", even_chrom);
               even_chrom = even_chrom+2;
         }
               exit(0);
   }
 printf("\n Enter chrom number less than 20 \n");
 }
```

OUTPUT

```
Enter chrom number
40

Enter chrom number less than 20

Enter chrom number
15

Even number of chromosomes are
2
4
```

```
6
8
10
12
14
```

THE DO–WHILE STATEMENT

The general format of a *do-while* iteration is

```
do
{
  statement block
} while (test condition)
```

The test condition is at the top in case of a `while` loop whereas it is at the bottom in a `do-while` loop.

Because the condition is tested at the end of the iteration, the statement block is executed at least once. This is very helpful in situations where it may be necessary for the body of the loop to be executed once before validating the test condition.

Once the test condition is satisfied, the block is executed again and it will continue to iterate till the condition is evaluated as false and the loop gets terminated.

Figure 3.6 shows the flow chart of the `do-while` statement.

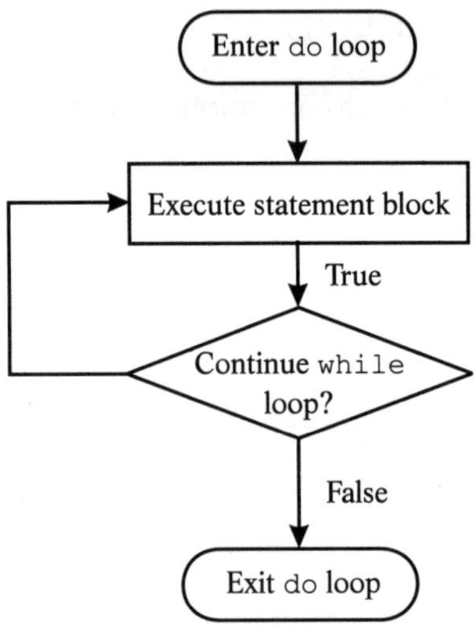

Fig. 3.6 The `do-while` flow chart

The `do-while` loop is less frequently used than the `while` and `for` loops. The program given below displays only characters denoting a member of the base pairs using the `do-while` loop.

PROGRAM 3.9: BASECHAR.C

```
#include <stdio.h>
main()
{
    char base, answer;

do {
  printf("\n Enter a base char in lower case \n");
  fflush(stdin);
  scanf("%c", &base);
  if(base != 'a' && base != 'g' && base != 't' &&
base !='c' && base!='u')
  {
        printf("\n Entered base char is invalid\
n");
  }
  else {printf("\n Entered base char is %c\n",
base); }

printf("\n Do you want to try again?\n");
fflush ( stdin);
scanf("%c", &answer);

} while (answer == 'y');
}
```

OUTPUT

```
Enter a base char in lower case
a

Entered base char is a

Do you want to try again?
y

Enter a base char in lower case
r

Entered base char is invalid

Do you want to try again?
n
```

THE BREAK STATEMENT: JUMPING OUT OF A LOOP

An exit from a loop can be achieved by invoking the `break` statement. When the break statement is encountered inside the loop, the loop is immediately exited and the program continues with the statement immediately following the loop. In case of nested loops, `break` would cause the program to exit from the loop that is containing it i.e. to say that if there are inner and outer loops, a `break` in the inner loop will not halt the execution of the outer loop.

THE CONTINUE STATEMENT: SKIPPING PART OF A LOOP

Sometimes it becomes necessary to skip a part of the statement block execution. The language C provides such functionality through its rich set of keywords. Unlike `break` which causes the loop to terminate, the `continue` statement causes the loop to `continue` with the next iteration by skipping all or any statement after it.
The general format of a `continue` statement is

```
continue;
```

The program given below uses `while`, `break` and `continue` statements to find the square root of residual values.

PROGRAM 3.10: SQRTRSDL.C

```
#include <stdio.h>
#include <math.h>
main()
{
/* To find the square root of residual values of
molecules */

int mol_no, loop_counter;
double residual_value, residual_sqrt;
loop_counter = 1;

while (loop_counter < 3)
{
       printf("\n Enter a molecule number \n");
  scanf("%d", &mol_no);
              if ( mol_no < 0)
  {
        printf("\n  Molecule number should always be
positive\n");
```

```
        break; /* end the loop */
  }

printf("\n Enter residual value for the given
molecule number \n");

scanf("%lf", &residual_value);
              if ( residual_value < 0)
{
  printf("\n Enter positive molecule number for
finding the sqrt \n");
  continue; /* Go to the beginning of the while loop
*/
  }

residual_sqrt = sqrt(residual_value);
printf("\n SQRT of residual value: %lf <for the
molecule number %d> is %lf \n", residual_value,
mol_no, residual_sqrt );

  loop_counter ++;
  }
}
```

OUTPUT

```
Enter molecule number <Range ?>
100

Enter residual value for the given molecule number
10
SQRT of residual value: 10.000000 <for the molecule
number 100> is 3.162278

Enter molecule number <Range ?>
40

Enter residual value for the given molecule number
23

SQRT of residual value: 23.000000 <for the molecule
number 40> is 4.795832
```

Chapter 4

Functions

A function is nothing but a sub-program that can perform a particular task. Functions help to break a large task into several smaller tasks. Therefore, the whole program consists of many small functions. The language C has been developed in such way that functions designed for one program can be reused in other programs to perform similar tasks.

Definition A function can be defined as being independent, having a name and performing a specific task or job.

Function Types

There are two kinds of functions.

1. Built-in functions
2. User-defined functions

Built-in Functions

These are the functions which are already predefined by C. They are built into the system and are ready for use by the user community.

Example: `printf, scanf, main etc.`

User-defined Functions

All functions other than the built-in functions are known as *user-defined functions*. These functions are developed by the user to perform certain tasks as per his/her needs. A function cannot be defined within another function. All user-defined functions can be compiled separately and have well-controlled entry and exit operations.

PROGRAM 3.10 in the previous chapter can be decomposed as shown in Fig. 4.1.

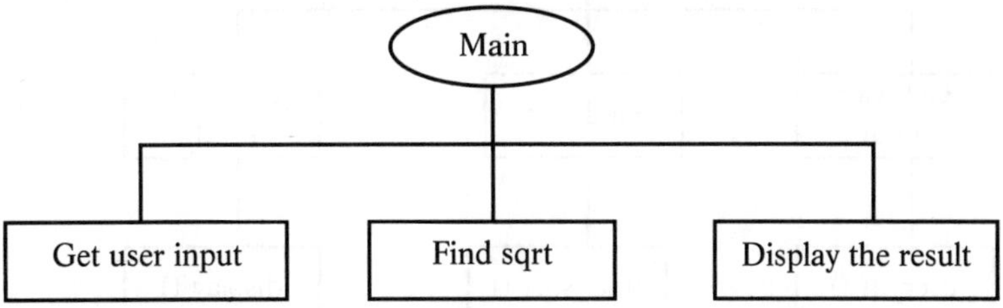

Fig. 4.1 Functional decomposition

The three main things that the program does is

1. Get user input: Obtaining molecule numbers and residual values from the user.
2. Find sqrt: Processing the user input and finding the square root of residual values. If the processing is complex, this can be further decomposed into smaller tasks resulting in more functions
3. Display result: Finally, displaying all results

Let us consider a further decomposition of Fig. 4.1. We can break each of the major functions of obtaining input, calculating square root and displaying the result, into smaller functions. For example 'find sqrt' is broken down to first finding the sqrt and then incrementing the value. This is shown in Fig. 4.2.

FUNCTION PROTOTYPE

Like the function header, the prototype includes function information namely `return type` (the type of variable that is passed back to the main program by the function), the function name and `arguments`. The normal practice is to place the prototype definitions of all functions before the main function.

The general format of a function is

```
<return type> <function name> (data type argument
1,…. ,data type argument n)
```

It is not very necessary to specify the parameter or argument names in the declaration, but the data type and its order are important. If the

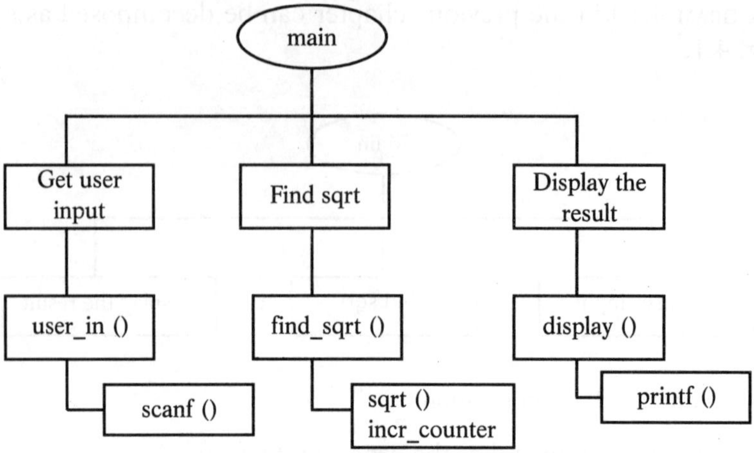

Fig. 4.2 Next level of decomposition

`<return type>` of a function is not declared, the C compiler assumes that the function will return an integer which might not always be true. Therefore, it is bad programming practice to avoid the `<return type>` in the declaration.

CALLING FUNCTIONS

Every program must contain one function named `main` where the program begins execution. The main may *call* other functions, which in turn may call some more. When a function is called, the program execution is transferred to the first statement in the called function. The function is completed when it executes the last statement in the function or it executes the return statement. After a function returns to the calling function, the program flow continues with the evaluation of the expression in which the call was made.

The general syntax to call a function is as given below

```
<function name> (arg1, arg2,…)
```

The syntax of `return` is very straightforward too:

```
return (expression);
```

There are two ways a function can be called:

1. by using its name and argument list in a statement (in such a case, the return value is discarded)
2. by calling a function in an expression (here the function evaluates up to a value i.e., return value)

Some calling functions may be from a standard library; some may be unique to the program; and some may be shared across many functions. The calling structure and variable scope (refer to the next section) not only facilitate reuse but also encourage modularity.

As discussed earlier, if PROGRAM 3.10 is decomposed, it can be represented to show case the modularity of the program using functions. Figure 4.3 shows the modular structure of the program.

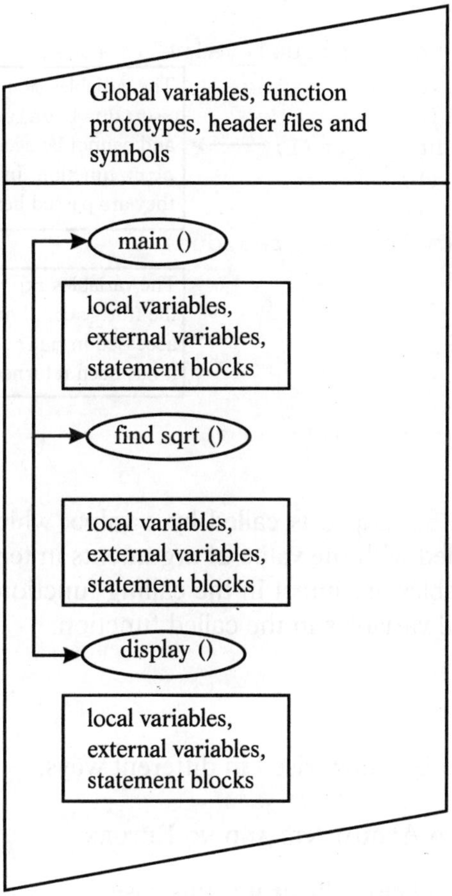

Fig. 4.3 Modular structure of PROGRAM 3.10

VARIABLE SCOPE

Functions communicate in two ways

1. through arguments or parameter lists and
2. through global variables

When a variable is declared within a function, it is local to that given function and cannot be accepted by any other outside function. In order to access the local variable in a given function by an outside function, it is necessary to pass the local variable as a parameter or an argument or to return the local variable to the outside function.

EXAMPLE

```
main()
{
  int mol_no, residual_value, value;
  . . . . . . . .
  user_in ();
  value = find_sqrt(); ──►
  display ();
}
```

> The variables `mol_no` and `residual_value` are local to `main` and cannot be accessed in the `find_sqrt` function. In order to access them, they are passed here as an argument

```
find_sqrt (molecule, residue)
{
  int counter;
  int sqrt_val;        ──►
  . . . . . .
  . . . . . .
  return (sqrt_val);
}
```

> The variables `sqrt_val` is local to the `find_sqrt` function and cannot be accessed in `main`. In order to access it, it has been returned here.

The function `find_sqrt` is called by a value, which means that the function is provided with the value of arguments in temporary variables. The original variables are intact in the calling function. Calling by value initialises the local variables in the called function.

ARGUMENTS

Function calls can be categorised in different ways.

FUNCTIONS WITH NO ARGUMENTS AND NO RETURN

The program given below illustrates this case

PROGRAM 4.1: ADD_1.C

```
#include <stdio.h>
main ()
{
  rna_total ();
}
```

```
void rna_total ()
{
  int rrna, trna, mrna, total;
  printf ("\n Enter three RNA numbers\n");
  scanf ("%d %d %d", &rrna, &trna, &mrna);
  total =  rrna + trna + mrna;
  printf ("\n Total RNA molecules are %d\n", total);
}
```

OUTPUT

```
Enter three RNA numbers
20
30
40

Total RNA molecules are   90
```

WITH ARGUMENTS AND NO RETURN

PROGRAM 4.1 can be modified in such a way that the numbers to be added are passed to the function as arguments to perform the addition.

PROGRAM 4.2: ADD_2.C

```
#include <stdio.h>
void rna_total(int,int,int);
main ()
{
  int rrna, trna, mrna;
  printf ("\n Enter three RNA numbers\n");
  scanf ("%d %d %d", &rrna, &trna, &mrna);
  rna_total (rrna, trna,mrna);
}

void rna_total(int rrna,int trna,int mrna)
{
  int total;

  total =  rrna_fn + trna_fn + mrna_fn;
  printf ("\n Total RNA molecules are %d\n", total);
}
```

Although the structure of the program is different, the output will be the same.

OUTPUT

```
Enter three RNA numbers
20
30
40

Total RNA molecules are   90
```

`rrna, trna, mrna` are automatic variables in `main` whose values are passed as an argument to `rna_total()` function. The variables `rrna, trna` and `mrna` are initialised to the values passed to them. The data type of variables a and b that are passed to rna_total() and the data type of the function variables `rrna, trna` and `mrna` which catch them should be the same.

WITH ARGUMENTS AND RETURN

In the above program, the function `rna_total()` can be modified to return the sum value, which can be displayed by the calling function.

PROGRAM 4.3: ADD_3.C

```
#include <stdio.h>
int rna_total(int,int,int);
main ()
{
  int total;
  int rrna, trna, mrna;
  printf ("\n Enter three RNA numbers\n");
  scanf ("%d %d %d", &rrna, &trna, &mrna);
  total = rna_total(rrna, trna,mrna);
  printf ("\n Total RNA molecules are %d\n", total);
}

int rna_total(int rrna,int trna,int mrna)
{
  int total;
  total =  rrna + trna + mrna;
  return(total);
}
```

OUTPUT

```
Enter three numbers
20
```

```
30
40

Total RNA molecules are  90
```

WITH NO ARGUMENTS AND RETURN

In PROGRAM 4.1, `rna_total()` function can be modified to return the sum that can be displayed in `main` function.

EXTERNAL VARIABLES

Unlike automatic variables, there are some variables which are defined outside all functions. Such variables are known as *external variables* and can be accessed by all functions. These variables are active throughout the execution phase of a program and are also known as *global variables*. As external variables are globally available, they can be used to communicate data instead of just passing on arguments. External variables are defined only once and used everywhere. They mainly help in communication, therefore, it is advisable not to rely too heavily on them—any unexpected modification of external variables would have adverse impact on the execution of the program.

PROGRAM 4.4: GBLLCL.C

```
#include <stdio.h>

/* The scope of the variable, peptide_len, is global
and can be accessed by all functions */
int peptide_len;

main()
{
/* Global variable is initialised to 10 */
peptide_len = 10;
printf("peptide length in main function is = %d\n",
peptide_len);
printf("peptide length in global function is = %d\
n", peptide_global());
printf("peptide length in local function is = %d\n",
peptide_local());
printf("peptide length in global function at second
iteration is = %d\n", peptide_global());
}
```

```
int peptide_global()
{
  /* Global variable is incremented by 10 */
  peptide_len += 10;
  return(peptide_len);
}

int peptide_local()
{
  /* The scope of this automatic variable is limited
to this function */
  int peptide_len;
  peptide_len = 1;
  return(peptide_len);
}
```

OUTPUT

```
peptide length in main function is 10
peptide length in global function is 20
peptide length in local  function is 1
peptide length in global function at second
iteration is 30
```

Thus, the global function of a variable, in this case, the peptide length, changes at every call.

STATIC VARIABLES

The word *static* refers to some thing that has no movement. Therefore, *static variables* are those whose values are retained even after the function exits. In a program, a variable becomes static by just adding the keyword '*static*' in front of the variable declaration. The value of the variable, when the function exits, will be retained until the next entry to the function.

In the program given below, the automatic variable is initialised to zero every time the function `auto_static` is called whereas the static variable retains its previous value upon every invocation of the function.

PROGRAM 4.5: NTSTATIC.C

```
#include <stdio.h>
void auto_static();
main ()
{
  int i;
```

```
  for ( i = 0; i < 5; ++i)
  {
        auto_static();
  }
}
void auto_static()
{
  int dna = 0;
  static int nt_number=0;/* number of nucleosides */

  printf("automatic = %d, static = %d \n", dna,
nt_number);

  ++ dna;
  ++nt_number;
}
```

OUTPUT

```
automatic = 0, static = 0
automatic = 0, static = 1
automatic = 0, static = 2
automatic = 0, static = 3
automatic = 0, static = 4
```

RECURSION

The C language supports a feature known as *recursive function.* Recursion is a method of calling a function in which the function being called (directly or indirectly) is the function itself.

Direct recursion A function `a()` contains a statement to call function `a()` itself

Indirect recursion A function `a()` calls function `b()` which in turn calls function `a()`

Recursive functions help in solving problems involving searching and sorting data efficiently. An example of how a recursive function works is illustrated below.

PROGRAM 4.6: RECURSION.C

```
/*
Prints values of restriction enzyme (RE) sites
recursively based on its initial value.
*/
```

```
#include <stdio.h>
#define MAX_COUNT_VALUE 10
int count (int);

main (argc, argv)
int argc;
char *argv[];
{
  int RE, result;
  if( argc !=2)
  {
        printf ("Usage: recursion <RE sites> \n");
        exit (0);
  }
  RE = atoi (*++argv);
  result = count (RE);
}

int count (re)
int re;
{
  printf(" RE site number : %d\n", re);
  while ( re > 0 )
  {
        if (re >= MAX_COUNT_VALUE)
        {
              return(re);
        }
        else
        {
              re = re+1;
              return ( count(re));
        }
  }
}
```

OUTPUT

```
Recursion

Usage:  recursion <RE Sites>

Recursion 5
RE site number: 5
RE site number: 6
RE site number: 7
RE site number: 8
RE site number: 9
```

```
RE site number: 10
```

When a function invokes itself recursively, each invocation gets a fresh set of automatic variables independent of the previous invocation. The count function is given 5 in the first invocation and receives a value incremented by one in subsequent invocations.

Some more examples of functions that can be implemented using recursion are `qsort`, `factorial` and even windows `login` functions.

PREPROCESSORS

The *preprocessor* is a unique language feature that processes a code before it passes through the compiler. It recognises special statements such as

1. `#include`: to include files
2. `#define`: to replace a symbolic name by a constant or test

Preprocessor statements are identified by the presence of the pound sign '#', which must be the first character in the statement. Preprocessor directives are placed in the source program before the `main` function.

A set of commonly used preprocessor directives and their functions are given in Table 4.1.

Table 4.1 Preprocessor directives

Directive	Function
`#define`	defines macro substitution
`#undef`	un-defines a macro
`#include`	specifies the files to be included
`#ifdef`	tests for a macro definition
`#endif`	specifies the end of #if
`#ifndef`	tests whether a macro is not defined
`#if`	tests a compile time condition
`#else`	specifies alternatives when a #test fails

MACRO SUBSTITUTION

Macro substitution is the process of replacing an identifier in a program by a pre-defined string. The directive used is '`define`' and the general format of a definition is

```
#define <identifier> <replacement text>
```

The replacement text is arbitrary. No semicolon appears at the end of the statement. A defined name or identifier is not a variable and therefore, it is not possible to assign a value to it. Any occurrence of the identifier in the source program is substituted with the replacement text by the preprocessor. The scope of the identifier defined by `#define` is from the point where it is defined to the end of the source program.

EXAMPLE

```
#define TRUE 1
#define FALSE 0
```

In the above statements, `TRUE` is defined and made equivalent to 1 and `FALSE` to 0. Now `TRUE` can be used anywhere in the program where the constant 1 is used.

Macro substitution helps make a program easy to read, easy to modify, portable and more efficient in terms of extendibility. It is possible to define expressions other than just simple constants and macros with arguments as well.

EXAMPLE

```
#define    TWO_PI            2*3.1415 (expression)
#define    square(x)         x*x (macro with arguments)
```

Some more examples of macros are given below:

```
#define    MAX(a,b)          ((a) > (b) ? (a): (b))
#define    bioprint(expr)    printf(#expr "=%d\n",expr)
```

THE ADVANTAGES OF FUNCTIONS

Functions provide many advantages. As explained in the beginning, they help in dividing a large task into a group of manageable tasks. Functions with a limited code size are easy to maintain and can also be easily re-used in other programs. All similar functions can be grouped together and put into a library for easy access. To access any function in the library, the program under compilation must specify the library at the time of compile/link phase.

Chapter 5

Character Input and Output

A character is a unit of information that corresponds to a symbol in the written form of any language. It can be a single alphabet, numeral, punctuation mark or any symbol from the *ASCII character set* (ASCII is a sequential formula for representing English characters as numbers, with each letter assigned a number from 0 to 127).

When a character is stored in memory, its ASCII code is put in memory—this is because there is no way to store characters directly in memory. A sequence of characters is called a *string*.

The program given below prints the amino acid (aa) singlet codes (a to t) along with their ASCII values.

PROGRAM 5.1: PRINTAA.C

```
#include <stdio.h>
unsigned char alphabet;
main()
{
  printf("\nAmino acid\t Singlet code\n\n");
  for (alphabet = 97; alphabet < 117; alphabet++)
  {
        if(alphabet == 98 ||alphabet == 106 ||
alphabet == 111 || alphabet == 98) continue;
        printf(" %c\t\t  %d\n", alphabet, alphabet);
  }
  return;
}
```

OUTPUT

```
Amino acid        ASCII
Singlet code      value
     a              97
     c              99
     d             100
     e             101
     f             102
     g             103
     h             104
     i             105
     k             107
     l             108
     m             109
     n             110
     p             112
     q             113
     r             114
     s             115
     t             116
```

The standard library in C language provides functions like `getchar` and `putchar` to read or write one character at a time during input/output operations.

READING A CHARACTER

A single character is read using the *`getchar`* built-in function. `getchar` takes the following form

```
variable name = getchar();
```

In the program given below, the value for variable aa (amino acid) is obtained through character input and displayed on the screen.

PROGRAM 5.2: GETAA.C

```
#include <stdio.h>
main()
{
  char aa;
  printf("Enter singlet code for aa\n");
  aa = getchar();
  printf("Entered aa is %c\n",aa);
}
```

OUTPUT

```
Enter singlet code for aa
a

Entered aa is a
```

WRITING A CHARACTER

A function analogous to `getchar` is used to write characters one at a time to the display device. The function is called *putchar*.

The general form is

```
putchar (i)
```

This function prints the contents of the integer variable 'i' as a character, usually on the screen. PROGRAM 5.2 can be modified to use `putchar` instead of `printf` to display the value of the character.

CHARACTER STRINGS

A string is an array of characters. It is a structured data type in its own right with its own characteristics. A string is highly dynamic in terms of length and configuration and this feature of the string makes it different from a simple array. For example, a string variable can contain a DNA sequence 'attgccatt' with a length of 9 characters at one point of time, but it may also hold 'RNA' with a length of 3 characters at another time.

A character string has no special declaration format; it is simply declared as an array of characters as shown below.

```
char <string name> [size];
```

where

`string name` is the variable identifier and

`size` is an integer value indicating the maximum number of characters the string can hold

Therefore, the declaration

```
char dna[10];
```

will accept a maximum of 9 DNA sequence characters and one character reserved to denote the end of the string.

EXAMPLE: `'attgccatt'` string will have

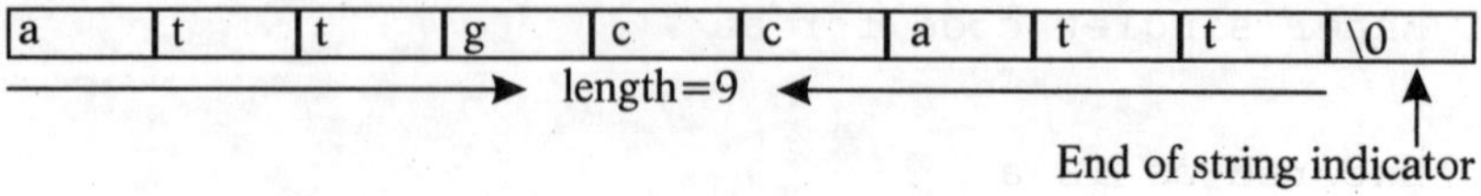

The C language provides many built-in functions which operate on strings. Some of these functions are shown in Table 5.1.

Table 5.1 String functions

Function	Description
`gets`(variable name)	accepts a string and stores it in the variable specified
`puts`(variable name)	prints the string stored in the variable
`strcpy`(str1,str2)	copies the string stored in `str2` to `str1`
`strcat`(str1,str2)	combines the strings `str1` and `str2` and stores it in `str1`
`strlen`(variable name)	returns the length of the specified string
`strcmp`(str1,str2)	compares two strings and returns 0 if both strings are equal > 0 if `str1` is greater than `str2` < 0 if `str1` is less than `str2`
`strcmpi`(str1,str2)	compares two strings ignoring the case

READING AND WRITING STRINGS

We can read and write strings in two ways.

1. Using `scanf` and `printf`
2. Using the `gets` and `puts` built-in string functions

The key difference between `scanf` and `gets` is that `scanf` accepts user input with a format specifier. `gets` does not require one.

PROGRAM 5.3 uses both `scanf` and `gets` to accept the same input sequences from a user.

Observe the output of the program. The same sequence 'atgcatgc' is entered for both calls; however `scanf` prints only 'atgc' while `gets` prints the whole sequence 'atgcatgc'. `scanf` accepts inputs based on the format or buffer full condition whereas `gets` accepts all inputs till a new line is encountered.

PROGRAM 5.3: GETSEQ.C

```
#include <stdio.h>
#include <string.h>

main()
{
  char seq1[20],seq2[20];

  printf("\n Enter bases in the DNA \n");
  scanf("%4s", &seq1);
  printf(" \n Retrieving sequences  with scanf
function %s\n",seq1);
  fflush(stdin);
  printf("\n Enter bases in the DNA \n");
  gets(seq2);
  printf(" \n Retrieving sequences  with gets
function %s\n",seq2);
  puts(seq2);
}
```

OUTPUT

```
Enter bases in the DNA
atgcatgc

Retrieving sequences with scanf function
atgc

Enter bases in the DNA
atgcatgc

Retrieving sequences with gets function
atgcatgc
```

Each character in a character array can be referred to using an index. The first character in the array is stored at index 0. Reading the array is done using a `for` loop. The `for` loop is terminated when the end of the string mark is reached—nothing but a null character.

The program given below obtains a sequence from the user and then prints one character at a time.

PROGRAM 5.4: STRCHAR.C

```
#include <stdio.h>
#include <string.h>

main()
{
char str[20];
int i;

printf("\n Enter any string \n");
gets(str);
for ( i=0;str[i] !='\0';i++)
{

  printf(" \n Char at position %d in the string:
%c\n" ,i, str[i]);
}
}
```

OUTPUT

```
Enter any string
bioinformatics

Char at position 0 in the string:   b

Char at position 1 in the string:  i

Char at position 2 in the string:  o

Char at position 3 in the string:  i

Char at position 4 in the string:  n

Char at position 5 in the string:  f

Char at position 6 in the string:  o

Char at position 7 in the string:  r

Char at position 8 in the string:  m

Char at position 9 in the string:  a

Char at position 10 in the string:  t

Char at position 11 in the string:  i

Char at position 12 in the string:  c

Char at position 13 in the string:  s
```

It is important to realise that two strings containing the same characters located between 'Z' and 'a' can be compared differently, depending on their case. For example, the two strings 'ENDONUCLEASE' and 'endonuclease' compare one way if the comparison is case sensitive and another way if the comparison is not. The example given below illustrates the comparison of upper and lower cases of the same string.

PROGRAM 5.5: STRCOMP.C

```
#include <stdio.h>
#include <string.h>
void comp_res(int);
main()
{
  char seq1[30],seq2[30];
  char str1[] = "ENDONUCLEASE";
  char str2[] = "endonuclease";
  int res;

  /* Case sensitive */
  printf("\n Case sensitive comparison of
ENDONUCLEASE and endonuclease\n\n");
  res = strcmp(str1,str2);
  comp_res(res);

  /* Case insensitive */
  printf("\n Case insensitive comparison of
ENDONUCLEASE and endonuclease\n\n");
  res = strcmpi(str1, str2 );
  comp_res(res);
}

void comp_res(int res)

{
if(res > 0)
        printf("ENDONUCLEASE is greater than
endonuclease\n" );
   else if(res < 0)
        printf("ENDONUCLEASE is less than
endonuclease\n" );
   else
printf("ENDONUCLEASE is equal to endonuclease\n");
}
```

OUTPUT

```
Case sensitive comparison of ENDONUCLEASE and
endonuclease

ENDONUCLEASE is less than endonuclease

Case insensitive comparison of ENDONUCLEASE and
endonuclease

ENDONUCLEASE is equal to endonuclease
```

Chapter 6

Arrays

An *array* is a collection of storage locations that have the same data type and name. Each storage location in an array is called an *array element*. There are two kinds of arrays.

1. *Static array* This kind of array contains a fixed number of elements and is allocated when the program is compiled.
2. *Dynamic array* This kind of array contains a dynamic number of elements decided by the dynamic memory management when the program is run. The array is resized as per requirement.

As with any data type, an array must be declared before it can be used. The general form of the declaration for a static array is

```
<data type> <array name> [maximum number of cells or
elements];
```

where

`data type`: any simple or structured data type except FILE
`array name`: any variable or identifier
`maximum number of cells or elements`: total number of locations in the array

Example

```
int orf[10]
char A4page[1024]
```

SINGLE-DIMENSIONAL ARRAYS

A single-dimensional array has only a single subscript. The subscript or index is used to identify an element in the array. The single-dimensional array consists of a set of contiguous memory locations and each location is accessed by an offset value from the first location. Each location or element in an array is accessed dynamically during program execution. Figure 6.1 shows a chunk of array data.

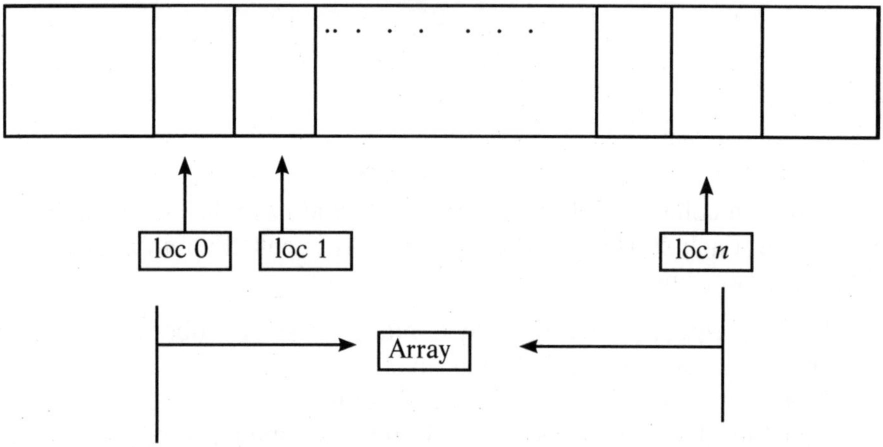

Fig. 6.1 Array of memory locations

INITIALISING ARRAYS

The elements of an array are initialised the same way as ordinary variables—when they are declared. It is possible to initialise all or part of an array at declaration. The general form of initialisation of an array is

```
(type) (array name) [size] = {list of values};
```

the values in the list are separated by commas.

EXAMPLE

```
int orf [6] = {30,40,50,60,70,20};
```

The above statement declares the variable `orf` as an array of size 6 and assigns values 30, 40, 50, 60, 70, 20 to the zeroeth, the first, second, . . . , fifth element. The number of initialised values must be equal to the number of array elements otherwise an error would be detected during compilation.

The program given below accepts values as the user types them in and displays all of them at the end using a character array buffer.

PROGRAM 6.1: CHARARR.C

```
/* A page has 24 lines and 80 characters per line.
Therefore, the maxium characters to hold in a buffer
is 24 × 80 */
#include <stdio.h>
main()
{
char ch;
int n = 0;
char A4page[1920];

printf("\nEnter characters to fill up an A4 page\n");
printf("\nPress <z> to end the entry\n");

/* The loop breaks when 'z' is pressed or n reaches
a max value */
while ( ((ch = getchar()) != 'z') && n < 1920)
{
  A4page[n++] = ch;
}
printf("\n Entered data is\n %s\n", A4page);
}
```

OUTPUT

```
Enter characters to fill up an A4 page

Press <z> to end the entry
z

Entered data is
z[1]
```

The program given below initialises an integer array and reads the values from the array. It then displays them on the user's screen.

PROGRAM 6.2: ORFARR.C

```
/* Declare an array containing the ORF[2] lengths of
various genes and initialise it */
```

---

1 This is only a sample output to test the program. We can type in any number of characters, but here we are keying in the last alphabet to terminate the program.

2 As you know ORF stands for an open reading frame, which is the part of an organism's genome containing the sequence of bases that could potentially encode a protein.

```
#include <stdio.h>
main()
{
int gene, orf[6] = {30,40,50,60,70,20};
/* Printing the array values */
for ( gene = 0; gene < 6; gene ++)
{
printf("\nLength of the ORF for gene %d is %d\n",
gene,orf[gene]);
}
}
```

OUTPUT

```
Length of the ORF for gene 0 is 30
Length of the ORF for gene 1 is 40
Length of the ORF for gene 2 is 50
Length of the ORF for gene 3 is 60
Length of the ORF for gene 4 is 70
Length of the ORF for gene 5 is 20
```

Program 6.3 defines a character array for nucleosides and initialises it with a, t, g and c. It also defines an integer array to hold the number of purines or pyramidines in a sequence. The user inputs the number of purines or pyramidines and these values are taken into the integer array. The program then displays the number of bases using both the character and integer arrays.

PROGRAM 6.3: NSARR.C

```
/*
Description: Displays the count of nucleosides
*/

#include <stdio.h>
main()
{
/* Declare an array to contain a t g c */

char base[4] = { 'a','t','g','c'}; /* nucleoside
array for a t g c */
int base_count[4]; /* array containing the count
values for nucleosides */
int count;
```

```
for (count=0; count<4; count++)
{
  printf("\nEnter number of '%c' nucleosides\n",
base[count]) ;
  scanf( "%d", &base_count[count]);
    fflush(stdin);
}
count = 0; /* Reinitialise the count as it's value
is 4 now */
for (count=0; count<4; count++)
{
  printf("\nNumber of bases of %c nucleosides are %d
\n", base[count],base_count[count]);
}
}
```

OUTPUT

```
Enter number of 'a' nucleosides
5

Enter number of 't' nucleosides
10

Enter number of 'g' nucleosides
12

Enter number of 'c' nucleosides
15

Number of 'a' nucleosides are 5

Number of 't' nucleosides are 10

Number of 'g' nucleosides are 12

Number of 'c' nucleosides are 15
```

MULTI-DIMENSIONAL ARRAYS

Unlike single-dimensional arrays, multi-dimensional arrays have more than one subscript. The number of subscripts depends upon the dimension of the array. In case of two-dimensional arrays, there are two subscripts. The data in a two-dimensional array are arranged in a row–column structure. The limit on the number of dimensions depends on the compiler. The general form of a multi-dimensional array is

```
(type) ( array name) [size1][size2]....[sizen];
```

where `size1` to `sizen` are the size of the respective dimensions.

The dimension `bio[i][j]` can be explained as below:

1. Take the address of `bio` and add `i`
2. The new address is `bio[0]+i` (say `bioi`)
3. Add `j` to the address `bioi` (say `bioij` is the new address)
4. Return the value at `bioij`

Figure 6.2 displays the arrangement of elements in a fixed size 3 × 3 two-dimensional array

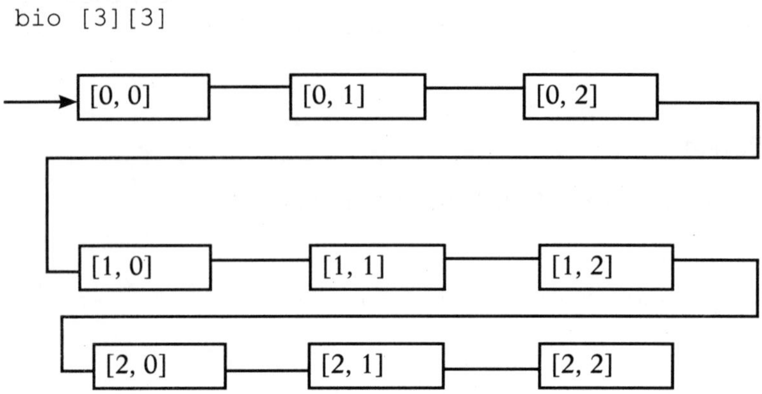

Fig. 6.2 Structure of a two-dimensional array

It is evident that in a two-dimensional array all the column elements are connected for a given row. Let us consider the two-dimensional matrix `bio[3][4]` given below.

$$\begin{pmatrix} r11 & r12 & r13 & r14 \\ r21 & r22 & r23 & r24 \\ r31 & r32 & r33 & r34 \end{pmatrix}$$

There are two ways the above matrix can be mapped to a single-dimension array:

1. Row major mapping
2. Column major mapping

Row Major Mapping

The 3 × 4 matrix mentioned above can be converted into a single-dimensional array *`biorow`* by collecting all the row elements. All the elements within a row should be collected from left to right and all the rows should be collected from top to bottom as is evident in Fig. 6.2. The new array *biorow* will be as given below:

row 0	row 1	row 2

```
biorow[] = [r11, r12, r13, r14, r21, r22, r23, r24,
r31, r32, r33, r34]
```

The `bio[i][j]` element can be located in *biorow* in the following manner:

`bio` has `i` rows and `j` columns (in the above example we have 3 rows and 4 columns).

Assume that each row has n elements and there are k rows to the left of row i. Therefore, there are $k \times n$ elements to the left of `bio[i][0]`.

Therefore, `bio[i][j]` is mapped to position $(k \times n + j)$ in the single-dimensional array *biorow*.

Now let us verify the above statement using the element `bio[2][3]` in *biorow*.

`n` = `4`: no of elements in each row
`k` = `1`: no of rows to the left of the 2nd row
`j` = `3`: the current column

Therefore, the position of `bio[2][3]` in array *biorow* is $4 \times 1 + 3 = 7$ i.e. it is the 7th element including the zeroth element, or the 6th element excluding the zeroth element in the array, which is `r23`.

`bio[3][2]` → $2 \times 4 + 2 = 10$ → 10th element in the array which is `r32`.

COLUMN MAJOR MAPPING

The illustrative 3 × 4 matrix `bio` used above can be converted into a single-dimensional array *biocol* by collecting all the column elements. The elements within a column should be collected from top to bottom and all columns should be collected from left to right. The new array *biocol* will be as given below:

```
biocol[] = [r11, r21, r31, r12, r22, r32, r13, r23,
r33, r14, r24, r34]
```

NOTE: Column major mapping does not access consecutive storage locations. Since we will be mainly using row major mapping in the examples mentioned in this book, column major mapping is not covered in detail.

The program given below uses two-dimensional arrays to display the biological activities of a solution in terms of the changes in molarity and normality.

PROGRAM 6.4:SOL.C

```
/*
Description : Displays the molarity and normality
for a given solution
*/

#include <stdio.h>
main()
{
int solution[2] = {1,2} ; /* array of solutions */
int M[2][2]; /* Molarity */
int N[2][2]; /* Normality */
int row, col ;

for (row=0; row<1; row++)
{
  printf("\nSolution number is %d \n",
solution[row]) ;
  for (col=0; col<2; col++) /* fills up the
activities for the given solution */
  {
      printf("\n Enter set %d <Molarity> value and
<Normality> value\n",col+1);
  scanf("%d %d", &M[row][col], &N[row][col]);
  }
}

/* Displays the molarity values for the given
solution */
for (row=0; row<1; row++)
{
  printf("\nMolarity values for solution %d\
n",solution[row]);
```

```
for (col=0; col<2; col++)   {
        printf("%dM\n",M[row][col]);
  }
}

/* Displays the normality values for the given
solution */

for (row=0; row<1; row++)
{
  printf("\nNormality values for solution %d\
n",solution[row]);
  for (col=0; col<2; col++)  {
        printf("\n%dN", N[row][col]);
  }
}
} /* End of the program */
```

OUTPUT

```
Solution number is 1

Enter set 1 <Molarity> value and <Normality> value
10
20

Enter set 2 <Molarity> value and <Normality> value
30
40

Molarity values for solution 1
10M
30M

Normality values for solution 1
20N
40N
```

Program 6.5 uses two-dimensional static arrays to build a matrix from two sequences inputted by the user. The program also illustrates the use of global variables and symbolic constants.

PROGRAM 6.5: BM.C

```
/*
To build a sequence matrix from a given sequence
*/
#include <stdio.h>
#include <stddef.h>
#define M_ROW 20
#define M_COL 20
void print_seq(int,int);
void build_seq_matrix();
int vseq(char s[]);
int seq[M_ROW][M_COL];  /* Global array with global
rows and column values */

main()
{
  build_seq_matrix();
}

void build_seq_matrix()
{
/* Builds seq matrix with given sequences and
initialises the first row and column with zeros */

int i,j,ret;
int row,col;
char seq1[15], seq2[15];


  printf("\n Enter the first DNA sequence \n");
gets(seq1);  /* Gets the first DNA sequence */
ret = vseq(seq1);
if( !ret) {
  printf("\nInvalid sequence\n");
  exit(0);
}
i = strlen(seq1);
ret=0;
  printf("\n Enter the second DNA sequence \n");
gets(seq2); /* Gets the second DNA sequence */
ret = vseq(seq2);
if( !ret) {
  printf("\nInvalid sequence\n");
  exit(0);
}
```

```
j= strlen(seq2);

if ( j> i ) {
  col = j+1;
  row = i+1;
}
else
{
  col = i+1;
  row = j+1;
}

/* Fills up the rest of the matrix with 1 s */
for (i=1; i <= row; i++)
{
  for (j=1; j <= col ; j++)  /* fills up the column
*/
  {
        seq[i][j] = 1;
  }

}
print_seq(row,col);
return;
}

void print_seq(int row, int col)
{
/* Sample seq1 is GAATTCAGTTA and Sample seq2 is
GGATCGA */
int i,j;

/* Prints the matrix from the first row and the first
column */
for (i=0; i  < row; i++)
{
  for (j=0; j < col ; j++)
  {
        printf( "%1d\t", seq[i][j] );
  }
                printf("\n");
}
return;
}
```

```
int vseq(char s[])
{
int i=0;
char base;
while (s[i] != '\0')
{
  base = islower(s[i]) ? toupper(s[i]) : s[i];
  if((base == 'G') || (base == 'A') || (base == 'C')
|| (base == 'T'))
  {
        ++i;
  }
  else return (0);
}
return(1);
}
```

OUTPUT

```
> bm
Enter the first DNA sequence
GAATTCAGTTA

Enter the second DNA sequence
GGATCGA

0   0   0   0   0   0   0   0   0   0   0   0
0   1   1   1   1   1   1   1   1   1   1   1
0   1   1   1   1   1   1   1   1   1   1   1
0   1   1   1   1   1   1   1   1   1   1   1
0   1   1   1   1   1   1   1   1   1   1   1
0   1   1   1   1   1   1   1   1   1   1   1
0   1   1   1   1   1   1   1   1   1   1   1
0   1   1   1   1   1   1   1   1   1   1   1

>bm

Enter the first DNA sequence
GAATTDAGTTA

Invalid sequence
```

Chapter 7

Pointers

Each location in the computer memory is uniquely identified by its address. As explained in Chapter 1, a variable points to a memory location. A *pointer* is a variable that contains the address of another variable. In other words, it is nothing more than the address of a memory location. A pointer operates on the concept of *indirection*.

Like all other variable declarations, a pointer variable too should be declared before use as shown below:

```
type name) *(variable name)
```

where

`type name`: simple or structured data type
`variable name`: name of the pointer variable
`*`: indicates that the variable is of a type pointer to a type name

Suppose we define a variable called `count` as follows.

```
int count = 10;
```

We can define another variable called `pcount` that can indirectly access the value of `count` by the declaration

```
int *pcount;
```

The unary operator, `&`, known as the *address operator* is used to make a pointer to an object. The statement given below uses the above variables to setup the indirect reference of count.

```
pcount = &count;
```

Therefore, it is important to note that there are two fundamental operators in pointers.

1. The address operator &
2. The indirection operator *

Figure 7.1 shows the indirection to an integer.

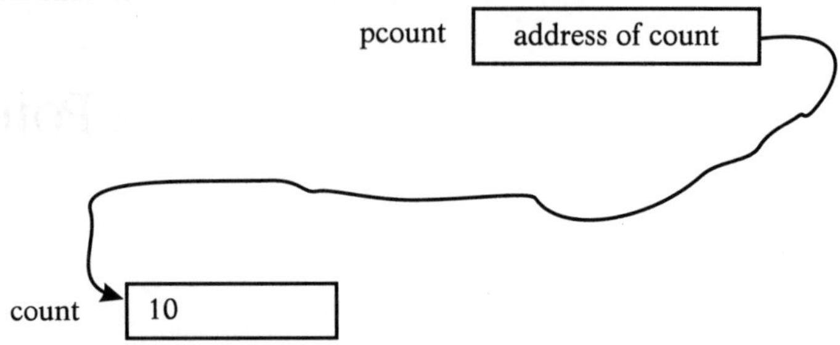

Fig. 7.1 Pointer to an integer

Always note that the type of the pointer and the variables it is pointing to should be the same. Some more examples of pointer definitions are given below.

```
int i, *i_ptr;
long x, *l_ptr;
char c, *c_ptr;
float f, *f_ptr;
double d, *d_ptr;
```

PROGRAM 7.1 illustrates the concept of pointer indirection.

PROGRAM 7.1: POINTER.C

```
#include <stdio.h>
main()
{
int pH, *pH_ptr;
pH= 5;
pH_ptr = &pH;

printf("Value of pH = %d\n", pH);
printf("Value of pointer to pH = %d\n", *pH_ptr);

printf("Address of pH = %x\n", &pH);
printf("Address in the pointer variable = %x\n", pH_
ptr);

*pH_ptr = 10; /* Change the value pointed to by
pH_ptr */
```

```
printf("Value of pH = %d\n", pH);
printf("Value of pointer to pH = %d\n", *pH_ptr);
}
```

In the above program, an integer variable `pH` and a pointer to it, `pH_ptr` are declared. The address of the variable `pH` is assigned to `pH_ptr` which means that both `pH` and `*pH_ptr` refer to the same memory location. Therefore, `pH` and `*pH_ptr` point to the same value. If the value in `pH_ptr` is changed, this change is passed on to the variable `pH`. Please verify the program output to understand the indirection.

OUTPUT

```
Value of pH = 5
Value of pointer to pH = 5
Address of pH = fff4
Address in the pointer variable = fff4
Value of pH = 10
Value of pointer to pH = 10
```

Figure 7.2 illustrates graphically what PROGRAM 7.1 actually does.

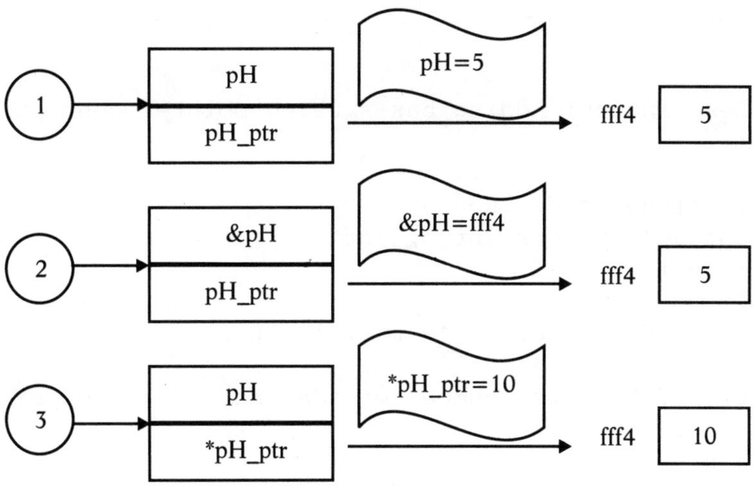

Fig. 7.2 Using indirection to access data

1: `pH` and `*pH_ptr` are defined in the program. The value is stored in the memory location `fff4`

2: The address of `pH` and the value of the pointer are the same, as `pH` is assigned to the pointer. The pointer accesses data from location `fff4`

3: The value at indirection is set to 10

It is important to note that the address operator `&` is complement to the indirection `*` operator. `*pH_ptr` specifies that the value at this location is an address and uses this address to access the desired value.

The pointer function gives us another method to pass values on to functions. Thus, the argument to a function can be passed in two ways:

1. *By value* In this case, the value of a variable from the calling function is copied to the variable in the called function and the original value of the variable in the calling function remains intact.
2. *By reference* In this case, where pointers are used, only the variable address is passed to the called function so that the calling and the called function variable point to the same location. Any changes made to the variable in the called function gets reflected in the calling function; that is say, the original value of the variable is modified.

The program given below adds residue values using pointers. The addresses of `a` and `t` are passed to the `add_numbers` function and the function returns the sum of the values referenced by the pointers.

PROGRAM 7.1: ADDNUM.C

```
/*
Description: Adding bases using pointer concepts
*/

#include <stdio.h>
int add_numbers(int *, int *);
main()
{
int a,t,basetotal, *a_ptr, *t_ptr;

printf("\nEnter number of adenine <A> residues\n");
scanf("%d", &a);
a_ptr = &a;

printf("\nEnter number of thymine <T> residues\n");
scanf("%d", &t);
t_ptr = &t;

basetotal = add_numbers(&a,&t);
printf("\nSum of a and t is %d\n", basetotal);
}
```

```
int add_numbers(int *a,int *b)
{
int c;
c = ( *a + *b );
return(c);
}
```

OUTPUT

```
Enter number of adenine <A> residues
23

Enter number of thymine <T> residues
23

Sum of a and t is 46
```

POINTERS AND ARRAYS

There is a close relationship between pointers and arrays. Any operation which can be achieved by array subscripting can also be done with pointers. Pointer arithmetic is faster than array indexing. If an array `seq[]` is declared then `seq` is the address of the first element or `&seq[0]` represents the address of its first element.

```
char seq[50], *pseq;
```

In the above statement, a sequence array `seq` of length 50 characters and a char pointer `pseq` are declared. The pointer can be initialised to the address of the first element of array `seq[]` in the following manner.

```
pseq = &seq[0];
```

As the array pointer is variable, it is easy to point it to any element in the array and modify the contents it points to.

POINTER ARITHMETICS

The pointer `pseq` in the above statement points to the first element in the array. To access the next element in the array, the pointer should be incremented so that it can point to the next element for access. The two most common operations on pointers are increments and decrements. When a pointer is increased or decreased, the pointer value increases or decreases by the size of the data type, thus pointing to an element up or down the array.

INCREMENTING POINTER

The increment operator increases the value of the pointer by 1 which means that the pointer points to the next storage location. In case of an array, it points to the next array element.

pseq++ value of the pointer is increased by the size of a char (1 byte) as each element in the array is of the char type. Suppose `pseq` is an integer pointer then
pseq++ the pointer is increased by the size of an int (2 bytes)

DECREMENTING POINTER

Decrementing a pointer is nothing but incrementing the pointer by a negative value. A decrement operator decreases the value by one.

pseq-- The value of the pointer is decreased by the size of a char (1 byte) as each element in the array is of char type
pseq-- The pointer is decreased by the size of an int (2 bytes) as `pseq` is an integer pointer.

Figure 7.3 shows how a pointer is scaled up in an array of locations.

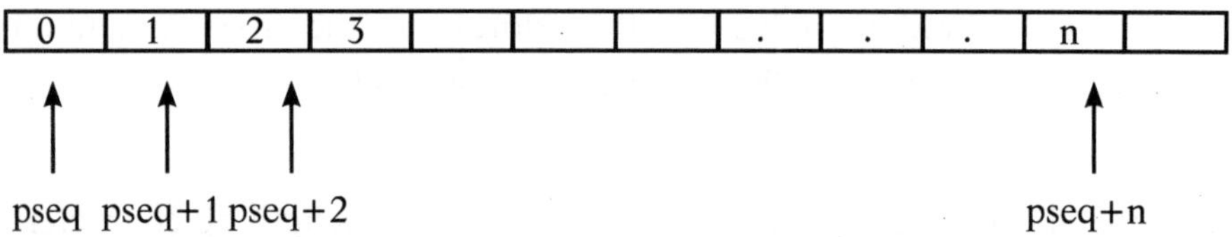

Fig. 7.3 Pointer operation

Some important pointer operations and the arithmetic involved are briefly explained in Table 7.1. These are very common and widely used operations in pointers.

Table 7.1 Pointer operations

Statement	Description
`++*seq`	Incrementing the value of the variable contained by `seq`. It is equivalent to `*seq = *seq+1`.
`*seq++`	Takes the value of the variable contained by `seq`. and then increments the address of `seq` by one. It is equivalent to `*seq ; seq = seq+1`.
`(*seq)++`	This is equivalent to `s = *seq; s= s+1`.
`*++seq`	This is equivalent to `++seq, *seq`.

The program given below illustrates the use of pointer arithmetics.

PROGRAM 7.2: ATHMTIC.C

```
/* Demonstration of pointer arithmetic */
#include <stdio.h>
#define MAX 10
main()
{
/* Declare and initialise an integer array */
int seqno[MAX] = { 10,11,12,13,14,15,16,17,18,19};

/* Declare an integer pointer and an integer*/
int *pseqno, seqcount;

/* Initialise the pointers */
pseqno = seqno;

/* Print the array elements using pointer arithmetic
*/

for(seqcount=0; seqcount<MAX; seqcount++)
{
printf("Element at %d\t: %d\n", seqcount,*pseqno++);
}
}
```

OUTPUT

```
Element at 0: 10
Element at 1: 11
Element at 2: 12
Element at 3: 13
Element at 4: 14
Element at 5: 15
Element at 6: 16
Element at 7: 17
Element at 8: 18
Element at 9: 19
```

PROGRAM 7.3 also demonstrates pointer operation and pointer arithmetics. Please note that the seq pointer is incremented by the length of the string sequence and that each pointer is de-referenced before assigning it to the array element for reversing the string.

PROGRAM 7.3: REVERSE_SEQ.C

```
/*
The given sequence is reversed from right to left.
Assume that the given sequence is GAATTCAGTTA;
then the reversed sequence should be ATTGACTTAAG.
Add validation logic to validate seq chars i.e.
validating ATGC chars in the stream.
*/

#include <stdio.h>
void reverse_seq(char *);
main()
{
char seq[50],*rev_seq;
printf("Enter a sequence with <length less than 20>\
n");
scanf("%s", &seq);
reverse_seq( &seq[0]);
}

void reverse_seq(char * seq)
{
int len = strlen(seq);
int i, j=0;
char rev_seq[50];
seq = seq+len-1;
for(i=len; i>0; i--)
{
  rev_seq[j++] = *seq--;
}
rev_seq[j] = '\0';

printf("Reverse sequence is %s\n", rev_seq);

return;
}
```

OUTPUT

```
Enter a sequence with <length less than 20>
GAATTCAGTTA

Reverse sequence is ATTGACTTAAG
```

POINTER AND FUNCTIONS

The C language supports pointers to functions. The general syntax is

```
<type> <(*function pointer)>();
```

In the above declaration, the pointer to the function returns the data type and the parenthesis around the function pointer are required.

A function pointer[1] (say `fptr`) can be used in PROGRAM 7.3 to the function `reverse_seq()`. The pointer can be initialised as

```
fptr = reverse_seq;
```

The program given below explains how to swap two given sequences using pointers.

PROGRAM 7.4: SWAPSEQ.C

```
/*
This program swaps the bases in a given even
sequence of bases. Assume that the sequence is
ATGCATGC. No sequence validation logic is included
in the program. It will swap every two bases in the
above sequence ie, the swapped sequence is TACGTACG.
The program assumes that the sequence has even
number of bases. If the sequence has an odd number
of bases, then the last base in the sequence is
truncated during the swap.
*/

#include <stdio.h>
int get_seq(char *);
char *swap_sequence(char *, char *);

main()
{
int len;
char sequence[132],sw_seq[132];

len = get_seq(&sequence);
printf("\nsequence is %s\n", sequence);
printf("\nsequence length is %d\n",len);
swap_sequence(&sequence[0],&sw_seq[0]);
}
```

---

[1] The use and demonstration of function pointers are not covered in detail in this text.

```
int get_seq(seq)
char *seq;
{
char input_seq[132];
printf("\nEnter a valid sequence\n\n");

gets(input_seq); /* Get the sequence from the user*/
strcpy(seq, input_seq);
return(strlen(seq));
}

char * swap_sequence(char * seq,char* swap_seq)
{

int oddflag =0,endswap=0,len = strlen(seq);
char *seq_ptr,f_char,s_char;
memset(swap_seq,'\0',(len+1));

if (*seq != NULL)
{
  seq_ptr = (char *)malloc( len+1);
  if (seq_ptr == NULL)
  {
        printf("Insufficient memory\n");
        return(NULL);
  }
  memset(seq_ptr,'\0',(len+1));
}
if( len % 2 !=0 ) oddflag=1;

while (*seq != NULL)
{
  if((len-endswap) == 1) break;
  f_char = toupper(*seq++);
  s_char = toupper(*seq++);
  *seq_ptr++ = s_char; /* Takes the value pointed by
seq */
  *seq_ptr++ = f_char;
  if(oddflag) endswap +=2;
}
if(oddflag)
{
  seq_ptr -= endswap;
  strncpy(swap_seq,seq_ptr,endswap);
}
```

```
else
{
  seq_ptr -= len;
  strncpy(swap_seq,seq_ptr,len);
}
free(seq_ptr);
printf("\nswapped sequence is %s\n", swap_seq);

return(swap_seq);
}
```

OUTPUT

RUN 1

```
Enter a valid sequence
atgcatgc

sequence is atgcatgc

sequence length is 8

swapped sequence is TACGTACG
```

RUN 2

```
Enter a valid sequence
atgcatgct

sequence is atgcatgct

sequence length is 9

swapped sequence is TACGTACG
```

The program given below will find the pattern 'atgc' in a given DNA sequence or sequences. It can be modified to find any pattern of your choice in any given sequence.

PROGRAM 7.5: PATTERN.C

```
/*
Finds the first occurrence of the pattern 'atgc' in a
given DNA sequence stream.
*/

#include <stdio.h>
#define MAX_SEQ_LEN 20
```

```
void find_pattern(char *);

main(argc, argv)
int argc;
char *argv[];
{

if(argc != 2) printf("Usage: pattern <seq1> <seq2>..
<seqn>\n");

while (-- argc) {
  find_pattern(*++argv);
  }
}

void find_pattern(char * s)
{
int i, len;
char seq[MAX_SEQ_LEN];

strcpy(seq, s);
len = strlen( seq);
printf("Seq for search is %s\n", seq);
if( strstr(seq,"atgc") != NULL) /* Finds the pattern
'atgc' in the string */
{
printf("pattern 'atgc' found\n");
printf("Seq length is %3d\n",len);
}
else printf("pattern 'atgc' not found \n");

return;
}
```

OUTPUT

```
pattern aattatgc
Seq for search is aattatgc
pattern 'atgc' found
Seq length is   8
```

Chapter 8

Structures

A *structure* is a collection or a group of variables—the variables can be of the same type or of different data types. A structure can also contain an array or another structure. The variables named in a structure are called *members*. A structure is declared by the C keyword `struct`. The general syntax of a structure is

```
struct <name of the structure>
{
  member-declaration
  member-declaration
  ...........
  ...........
} variable-list;
```

The begin and end braces help end the list of variables that are declared as members of the structure. The variables may be declared at the time that the structure is defined by listing them before the semi colon.

For example, the statement given below implies that X is a variable of type `struct dna`:

```
struct dna X;
```

while

```
struct dna *X;
```

means that X is a variable pointer to a structure of type `struct dna`.

The members of the structure can also be initialised in the same format as an array. For example, if we want to have the following structure, `human`, declared

```
struct human
{
int age;
char blood_grp;
char race;
};
```

it is possible to initialise the structure following its definition as

```
struct human = {35,'O','W'};
```

The operator '.' is a member operator of a structure. It basically connects the structure name and the member name. For example, 'human.race' indicates that the member race belongs to human structure.

Like variables, a structure variable can also be assigned to another variable of a similar type by its address with the & operator or by assigning its individual members to other variables. But unlike variables, structures cannot be compared.

The program given below demonstrates the use of structures. A structure dna is declared with its members and the member data keyed in by the user is taken into the structure and later displayed on the user's screen. The structures used in this program are defined in the dna.h file which is provided in the Appendix.

PROGRAM 8.1: DNASTRUC.C

```
/*
Description: Creates a structure for protein and
dna, accepts input from the user and displays its
values
*/

#include <stdio.h>
#include "dna.h"
int* find_basetotal(char *);
void input_protein();
void input_dna();
void display_protein(struct protein);

main()
{
input_protein();
input_dna();
}
void input_protein()
{
```

```
  struct protein ptn;

  printf("\nEnter aa type\n");
  scanf("%c",&ptn.aa_type);
  fflush(stdin);
  printf("Enter mass in daltons\n");
  scanf("%d",&ptn.mass);

  printf("Enter pKa < Less than 3>\n");
  scanf("%f",&ptn.pKa);

  fflush(stdin);
  display_protein(ptn);
  return;
}

/* It is possible to have more than one TATA in
a given DNA sequence. Use string manipulation
techniques to find the number of TATA in a sequence
and update TATA member variables in dna structure.
This is not done in this program.
*/
void input_dna()
{
char seq[100];
int base[4],*temp,tbase,ag,tc,i;
struct dna insulin;

/* Accept DNA data from the user and take them into
structure variables */

printf("\nEnter DNA sequence\n");
scanf("%s",&seq[0]);
fflush(stdin);
printf("\nEnter species type < Max length 9>\n");
scanf("%s",&insulin.organism);
insulin.seq_number = insulin.seq_number + 1;

/* The individual total of a,t,g,c in the input
sequence is returned into temp by find_basetotal
function */

temp = find_basetotal(&seq);
for(i=0;i<4;i++) {
        base[i] = *temp++;
}
```

```
/* Find out the number ag and tc in the given
sequence and the total number of bases in the input
sequence*/

tbase = base[0] + base[1] + base[2] + base[3];
ag = base[0] + base[2];
tc = base[1] + base[3];

if(tbase < 10)
{
  insulin.purines = 10 + ag;
  insulin.pyramidines = 10 + tc;
}
else
{
  insulin.purines = 100 + ag ;
  insulin.pyramidines = 100 + tc;
}
/* Displays the data using structure */

printf("\nPrinting DNA data from dna structure\n");
printf("\nSeq : %s \n", seq);
printf("nSpecies type : %s  \n",insulin.organism);

printf("\npurines : %d \t pyramidines : %d\n",
insulin.purines, insulin.pyramidines);

}

int* find_basetotal(char *seq)
{
char *s;
int i,a,t,g,c,len,base[4]= { 0,0,0,0};

s = seq;
len = strlen(s);

for(i=0;i<=len;i++)
{
/* Verify a,t,g, c nucleosides in the sequence and
find the total number of each using switch structure
*/
```

```
  switch((*s))
  {
        case 'a':
              base[0] += 1;
              break;
        case 't':
              base[1] += 1;
              break;
        case 'g':
              base[2] += 1;
              break;
        case 'c':
              base[3] += 1;
              break;
  }
  ++s;
  }
  return(&base);
  }

void display_protein(struct protein ptn)
{
printf("\nPrinting protein data from protein
structure \n");
printf("\n aa Type : %c \t Mass : %d \t pka : %f\
n",ptn.aa_type,ptn.mass,ptn.pka);
}
```

OUTPUT

```
Enter aa type
a

Enter mass in daltons
2

Enter pKa < Less than 3>
2

Printing protein data from protein structure
aa Type : a    Mass : 2    pKa : 2.000000

Enter DNA sequence
atgcaatg
```

```
Enter species type < Max length 9>
cat

Printing DNA data from dna structure

Seq : atgcaatg
nSpecies type : cat

purines : 15   pyramidines : 13
```

NESTED STRUCTURES

A structure can contain other structures that have their own members. For example, we can define a structure `human` that contain the above discussed `dna` structure as follows:[1]

```
struct human
{
struct dna insulin;
struct bg bgrp;
char race;
};
```

The new structure `human` will now have `insulin` structure as one of its members. The example given below briefly illustrates this using a structure that contains other structures. It is obvious that the `insulin`, `blood group` and `race` are different for different human objects. Please note that the program does not handle errors during the `scanf` function.

PROGRAM 8.2: NESTED.C

```
/*
Description: Demonstrates how to use nested
structures during data entry and processing
*/

#include <stdio.h>
#include "dna.h"
void input_insulin(struct human *);
struct human input_bg_details();
void display_bg_details(struct human);
char ans = 'N';
```

[1] The structure `bg` is defined in `dna.h` file in the Appendix

```
main()
{
struct human person;
person = input_bg_details();
if(person.bgrp.btype != NULL)
{
printf("Enter insulin details for blood type %c < Y
or N>?\n",person.bgrp.btype);
  fflush(stdin);
  scanf("%c",&ans);
  ans = toupper(ans);
  if(ans == 'Y') input_insulin(&person);
}
display_bg_details(person);

}
void display_bg_details(struct human person)
{

if(person.bgrp.btype != NULL)
{
printf(" The details for the blood type %c\n\
n",person.bgrp.btype);
  printf("Anti bodies: %c\t Anti gens: %c\t",person.
bgrp.ab,person.bgrp.ag);
  printf("Recipients: %s\tDonors: %s\n",person.bgrp.
rcpt,person.bgrp.donor);
  if(ans == 'Y') printf("\npurines : %d\
tpyramidines : %d\n",person.insulin.purines, person.
insulin.pyramidines);
}
}

struct human input_bg_details()
{
struct human ram;
char btype;

printf("Enter any blood type < A,B,O> \n");
fflush(stdin);
scanf("%c",&btype);

switch(toupper(btype))
{
  case 'A':
        ram.bgrp.btype = 'A';
        ram.bgrp.ab = 'B';
        ram.bgrp.ag = 'A';
```

```
        strcpy(ram.bgrp.rcpt,"O,A");
        strcpy(ram.bgrp.donor,"A,AB");
        break;
  case 'B':
        ram.bgrp.btype = 'B';
        ram.bgrp.ab = 'A';
        ram.bgrp.ag = 'B';
        strcpy(ram.bgrp.rcpt,"O,B");
        strcpy(ram.bgrp.donor,"B,AB");
        break;
  case 'O':
        ram.bgrp.btype = 'O';
        ram.bgrp.ab = 'B';
        ram.bgrp.ag = '\0';
        strcpy(ram.bgrp.rcpt,"O");
        strcpy(ram.bgrp.donor,"O,A,B,AB");
        break;
  default:
        break;
}
return(ram);
}

/* Enter insulin details for the blood type */

void input_insulin(struct human *person)
{
printf("\nEnter purines\n");
scanf("%d",&(person->insulin.purines));
printf("\nEnter pyramidines\n");
scanf("%d",&(person->insulin.pyramidines));
printf("\npyramidines = %d\n",person-
>insulin.pyramidines);

return;
}
```

OUTPUT

```
Enter any blood type < A,B,O>
A
Enter insulin details for blood type A < Y or N>?
Y

Enter purines
10
```

```
Enter pyramidines
20

The details for the blood type A
Anti bodies: B   Anti gens: A  Recipients: O,A
Donors: A,AB

purines: 10   pyramidines : 20
```

STRUCTURES AND ARRAYS

A structure can contain one or more arrays as members of the structure. For example,

```
typedef struct {
int maxr, maxc;
int m [2][2];
} matrix;
```

The above structure of matrix type has two integer members `maxr` and `maxc` which are nothing but the row and column variables and m a two-dimensional static array. The elements of the array are accessed as normal members using both member operator '.' and array index or subscripting. For example, `matrix.m[0][0]` points to the first element of the array. This expression is similar to a pointer to an `m[][]` array and therefore, the contents of the array can be printed on the display screen using standard calls like `puts` and `printf`.

The C language supports declaration of an array of structures. This is different from an array contained in a structure. Each element in an array of structures is a structure of the same type. In complex programming situations, arrays of structure can be very handy and powerful tools to solve intricate problems.

EXAMPLE

```
struct dna insulin[2];
```

`insulin` is an array of `dna` structures. Each array element `insulin[i]` is a dna structure and the members of the structures are accessed as follows

```
<array name[index].<member variable>
```

So, `insulin[0].purines` is a member variable in the first structure.

The program given below illustrates the relationship between structures and arrays. The main purpose of the program is to bring about a clear understanding of the concept and therefore, no validation of the sequence is done. It also does not handle errors.

PROGRAM 8.3: ARRSTRUC.C

```
/*
Shows an insulin array of dna structures and prints
a structure using a two-dimensional array.
*/
#include <stdio.h>
#include "dna.h"
void init_arrayof_structures();
matrix input_matrix();

main()
{
matrix res;
int i,j;
init_arrayof_structures();
res = input_matrix();

printf("\nPrinting matrix values from a structure
member\n");
for (i=0;i<(res.maxr);i++)
{
  for(j=0; j<(res.maxc); j++)
  {
        printf("%d \t",res.m[i][j]);
  }
  printf("\n");
}
}
void init_arrayof_structures()
{
struct dna insulin[2];
int j;
char seq[100];

for (j=0;j<2;j++)
{

/* Finds the number of purines and pyramidines */
printf("\nEnter no of purines in a DNA <A,B>
sequence\n");
scanf("%d",&insulin[j].purines);
```

```
printf("\nEnter no of pyramidines in a DNA <A,B>
sequence\n");
scanf("%d",&insulin[j].pyramidines);
}

printf("\n <A> purines : %d\t <A> pyramidines : %d\
n",insulin[0].purines, insulin[0].pyramidines);
printf("\n <B> purines : %d\t <B> pyramidines : %d\
n",insulin[1].purines, insulin[1].pyramidines);

}

matrix input_matrix()
{
matrix nt;
int i,j,ch;
static int count = 1;
nt.maxr = 2;
nt.maxc = 2;
printf("\n\n");
for (i=0;i<(nt.maxr);i++)
{
  for(j=0; j<(nt.maxc); j++)
  {
  printf("Enter element [%d] value \n",count++);
        scanf("%d",&ch);
        nt.m[i][j] = ch;
  }
}
return(nt);
}
```

OUTPUT

```
Enter no of purines in a DNA <A,B> sequence
8

Enter no of pyramidines in a DNA <A,B> sequence
10

Enter no of purines in a DNA <A,B> sequence
12

Enter No of pyramidines in a DNA <A,B> sequence
10
<A> purines : 8      <A> pyramidines : 10
```

```
<B> purines : 12     <B> pyramidines : 10

Enter element [1] value
2

Enter element [2] value
3

Enter element [3] value
4

Enter element [4] value
5

Printing matrix values from a structure member
2       3
4       5
```

STRUCTURE AND POINTERS

Pointers can also be used as members of the structure. The pointers declared inside a structure must be initialised with values before use. Both character pointers and character arrays reside simultaneously inside the structure, the key difference between them being that

1. An array is limited by its size at the time of declaration.
2. A pointer is limited by its external storage as it is initialised outside the structure. However, all that is pointed to by the pointer becomes part of the structure.

A C program supports declaration of a pointer to a structure in the same way as a pointer to an array. The general syntax for pointer declaration is

```
<struct keyword> <structure name> <pointer name>
```

EXAMPLE

```
strcut dna *pdna;
```

where `pdna` is a pointer of type `dna`. The pointer is initialised as follows

```
pdna = &dna;
```

The members of the structure can be accessed either by '.' or '->' member operators. Therefore, the member `purines` in `dna` can be accessed as

1. *dna->purines* This is the most common way of accessing structure members using pointer
2. *(*pdna).purines* This accesses members using the indirection of the pointer

The program given below defines a `date` structure and its members are initialised to date values. The structure `seqpara` contains integer pointers which point to the address of integer variables. The values of the pointers are printed using indirection. If the value in the pointer is changed, then the value in the variable too will be changed.

PROGRAM 8.4: SDATE.C

```
#include <stdio.h>
struct date
{
int day;
int month;
int year;
};

struct carbo
{
int *glucose;
int *sucrose;
}
main()
{
struct date anydate;
struct date *pdate;
struct carbo carbohyd;
int glucose, sucrose;

pdate = &anydate;

pdate->day = 10;
pdate->month = 2;
pdate->year = 2008;

printf("\n The date is %d-%d-%d\n",pdate->day
,pdate->month ,pdate->year);

glucose = 20;
sucrose = 6;
```

```
carbohyd.glucose = &glucose;
carbohyd.sucrose = &sucrose;

printf("\n\nGlucose mols = %d \t Sucrose mols = %d\
n",glucose,sucrose);
printf("\ncarbohyd.glucose = %d \t carbohyd.sucrose
=%d\n",*carbohyd.glucose,*carbohyd.sucrose);
}
```

OUTPUT

```
The date is 10-2-2008

Glucose mols = 20          Sucrose mols = 6
carbohyd.glucose = 20      carbohyd.sucrose = 6
```

PROGRAM 8.5 defines a page structure with the length, width of the page, the banner to be printed on the page and the pointer to hold the text keyed in by the user. The functions `nextline()` and `nextpage()` prints on the next line and the next page with the banner on the top respectively. `putline()` will print the same character on one complete line. For the sake of simplicity, it is assumed that the width of the page is 2 and the number of pages required to be printed are 2.

PROGRAM 8.5: SPAGE.C

```
#include <stdio.h>
#define PAGELENGH 4
#define PAGEWIDTH 80
#define NOPAGES 2

struct page
{
   int width;
   int length;
   char banner [100];
   char *biostr;
};

struct page *ppage;
void nextpage();
void nextline();
void putline(int);
int line_counter ;
```

```
int page_counter = 1;

main()
{
char biostr[80];
        int len,nopages;
struct page biopage;

ppage = &biopage;
ppage->width = PAGEWIDTH;
        ppage->length = PAGELENGH;
strcpy(ppage->banner,"Welcome to Bioinformatics");
nopages = NOPAGES;

nextpage();
len = ppage->length;
while(nopages-- > 0)
{
  if (len <=0 ) len = ppage->length;
  while(len-- > 0)
  {
        putline('A');
  }
}
printf("\n\n Enter a bio string into pointer\n");
gets(biostr);
ppage->biostr = biostr;
printf("\n\n Bio string is: %s\n", ppage->biostr);

}

/*
Print a newline and update line counter

*/
void nextline()
{
(void)putchar('\n');
line_counter++;
if(line_counter > ppage->length && ppage->length >
0)    nextpage();
}

/*
Take a new page on the output and print banner
*/
```

```
void    nextpage()
{
(void)putchar('\f');                              /*
Take new page        */
line_counter = 0;                             /* Print
page banner   */
(void)printf("\t  %s\t  Page %d", ppage->banner,
page_counter++);
nextline();
}

void putline(c)
int     c;
{
int n = ppage->width;
while(n-- > 0)
              (void)putchar(c);
nextline();
}
```

OUTPUT

```
Welcome to Bioinformatics   Page 1
AAAAAAAAAAAAAAAAAAAAAAAAAAAAAAAAAAAAAAAAAAAAAAAAAAAA
AAAAAAAAAAAAAAAAAAAAAAAAAAAA
AAAAAAAAAAAAAAAAAAAAAAAAAAAAAAAAAAAAAAAAAAAAAAAAAAAA
AAAAAAAAAAAAAAAAAAAAAAAAAAAA
AAAAAAAAAAAAAAAAAAAAAAAAAAAAAAAAAAAAAAAAAAAAAAAAAAAA
AAAAAAAAAAAAAAAAAAAAAAAAAAAA
AAAAAAAAAAAAAAAAAAAAAAAAAAAAAAAAAAAAAAAAAAAAAAAAAAAA
AAAAAAAAAAAAAAAAAAAAAAAAAAAA
```

```
Welcome to Bioinformatics   Page 2
AAAAAAAAAAAAAAAAAAAAAAAAAAAAAAAAAAAAAAAAAAAAAAAAAAAA
AAAAAAAAAAAAAAAAAAAAAAAAAAAA
AAAAAAAAAAAAAAAAAAAAAAAAAAAAAAAAAAAAAAAAAAAAAAAAAAAA
AAAAAAAAAAAAAAAAAAAAAAAAAAAA
AAAAAAAAAAAAAAAAAAAAAAAAAAAAAAAAAAAAAAAAAAAAAAAAAAAA
AAAAAAAAAAAAAAAAAAAAAAAAAAAA
AAAAAAAAAAAAAAAAAAAAAAAAAAAAAAAAAAAAAAAAAAAAAAAAAAAA
AAAAAAAAAAAAAAAAAAAAAAAAAAAA
```

```
Welcome to Bioinformatics   Page 3

Enter a bio string into pointer
this a bio string into a pointer contained in
structure

Bio string is: this a bio string into a pointer
contained in structure
```

Chapter 9

Files

The treatment of files in C is very simple unlike in other programming languages where there are special in-built and often rigid files structures and file handling routines. The C language treats file input/output in much the same way as any input/output statement from/to the terminal.

The simplicity of file input/output in C lies in the fact that it essentially treats a file as a stream of characters and accordingly allows input/output in streams of characters. Functions are available for all operations involving single characters, multiple characters input/output from/to files.

Opening Files

Stream files are opened in C using the `fopen` built-in function. The general syntax for opening a file is as follows

```
FILE *fopen(const char* filename, const char *mode);
```

The `fopen` function call returns a pointer variable of type `FILE`. The return pointer which is also called a *file pointer* is a pointer to the structure `FILE` and will have more information about the file. Refer to the `stdio.h` file[1] to understand more about `FILE` structure. If the file cannot be opened for any reason, the `fopen` call returns `NULL`. There are different modes of opening a file (Table 9.1).

---

1 Available in the Compiler used by your computer.

Mode	Description
`r`	File is opened for read only
`w`	File is opened for writing; all previous contents in the file are discarded
`a`	File is opened in the append mode i.e. writing can be done at the end of the file
`r+`	File is opened for reading and writing i.e. update
`w+`	File is opened to update but previous contents are discarded
`rb or w+b`	File is opened for reading or writing in binary

Table 9.1 File modes

For example, to open a `fasta` file, `dna.fas`, only to read sequences, the following statement can be used

```
FILE *dna_fp;
dna_fp = fopen("dna.fas","r");
```

Figure 9.1 shows a flow chart describing opening of files in C.

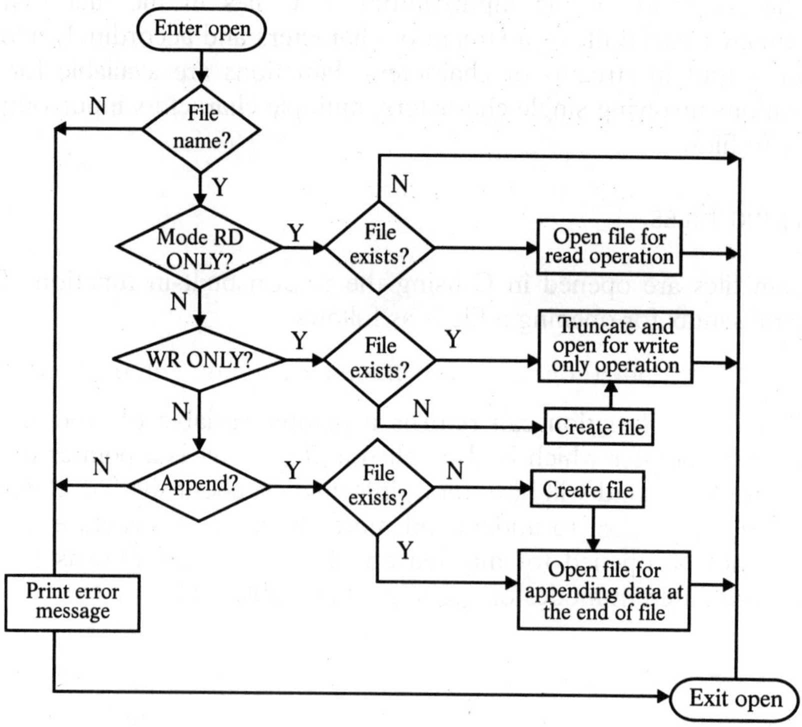

Fig. 9.1 Flow chart for opening files

The lengths of the filenames are different in different operating systems. In DOS, the filename format is

<8 chars *filename*.3chars *extension*>

whereas in other operating systems like UNIX, VMS etc the filename is more than 8 characters. The C language does not allow certain special chars (/ \ : * ? " < > |) to be part of the file name.

CLOSING FILES

When files are no longer needed for any operation, they should be closed. The prototype of the file close statement is given below.

```
int fclose(file pointer)
```

where `file pointer` refers to the `FILE` pointer of the open file.

For example, `dna.fas` sequence file is closed by

```
fclose(dna_fp);
```

Before closing the stream file, the `fclose()` call flushes any unwritten data and closes the file.

It is good programming practice to close all open files explicitly though the operating system does close all open files whenever a program terminates or in any unforeseen eventuality. The other reason to close an open file once it is done is that the number of files that can be open simultaneously is restricted by the operating system.

READ AND WRITE OPERATIONS

Read and write operations are done to files on the disc in the following ways

1. Formatted input/output to read/save data from/to disc file
2. Character input/output to read/save single characters or a stream of characters from/to a file
3. Direct input/output to read/save a block of the memory

FORMATTED OUTPUT

The `printf` function provides formatted output conversion. Consider the following statement.

```
int fprintf(FILE *file pointer, const char
*format, . . .)
```

The above function writes the data into a disc file using the file pointer and the format specifiers. It then returns the number of characters written, or displays a negative value to indicate an error.

The format specifier may have certain special signs as part of it during print conversion of data (Table 9.2).

Sign	Description
–	Left adjustment
+	Print a number with + sign
0	Field width is padded with leading zeros
.	Separates field width from precision
`number`	Max field precision during field printing

Table 9.2 Format specifier

The statement `int printf(const char* format)` is equivalent to `fprintf(stdout)`. Sometimes `sprintf` is also used to print data from a file. The format is as given below

```
int sprintf(char *s, const char *format, . . .)
```

`sprintf` is the same as `printf` except that the output is written into the string `s` and terminated with '\0'. `s` must be big enough to hold the result.

FORMATTED INPUT

To input data from a file, the built-in function call `fscanf` is used. It is similar to `scanf` except that `scanf` reads data from a standard input. The general format for `fscanf` is

```
int fscanf(FILE *fp, const char *format, . . .);
```

CHARACTER INPUT AND OUTPUT

The language C provides two built-in functions to accept and print characters, namely `getc` and `putc` with the variants `fgetc` and `fputc` for files.

The syntax for `getc` and `fgetc` are

```
<variable name of type char> = getc();
<variable name of type char> = getc(file pointer);
```

While the syntax for `fputc` and `putc` are

```
fputc(character variable, file pointer );
putc(character variable );
```

getc and fgetc work the same way; so does putc () and fputc (). The difference is that getc and putc use stdin and stdout file pointers for input and output operations.

Similarly, there are gets() and fgets() commands for string operations.

The syntax[2] for fgets is

```
char *fgets(char *string, int n, FILE *fp);
```

and for gets is

```
char gets(char *string);
```

The following program uses character i/o functions to accept characters from the user and put them into a file. We can read the text that is put into the file if the main program makes a call to the readfile() function which opens the text file and uses the getc() function call instead of the putc() call in a loop to read the file till the end.

PROGRAM 9.1: FILEIO.C

```
#include <stdio.h>
void writefile(char *fname);

main(argc,argv)
int argc;
char *argv[];
{
char fname[14];
if(argc !=2)
{
  printf("\n File required for read-write operation\
n");
  printf("\n Format : Fileio <filename>\n");
  exit(0);
}
if(strlen(argv[1]) > 13)
{
   printf("File name too long\n");
   printf("File name format: <xxxxxxxx.xxx>\n");
```

[2] Refer to C compiler help file for more information.

```
   exit(0);
  }
  else strcpy(fname, argv[1]);
  writefile(fname);
  printf("\n Reading the input file %s\n",fname);
  }

  void writefile(char *fname)
  {
  char c;
  FILE *fp;

  fp = fopen(fname,"w");

  printf("\n Enter the text to write to file\n");

  printf("\n Press <tilda ~ > to quit input\n");

  while(( c= getchar()) != 0x7e) /* terminate the loop
  on tilda */
  {
    putc(c,fp);
  }
  close(fp);
  }
```

OUTPUT

```
>fileio

File required for read-write operation

Format : Fileio <filename>

>fileio fi.txt

Enter the text to write to file

Press <tilda ~ > to quit input
this is a test
this is a test
~

>type fi.txt
this is a test
this is a test
```

DIRECT I/O

Direct input/output functions are used for low level I/O operations and for transferring blocks of data to and from a disc file. The direct I/O functions are `read ()` and `write ()`. The format in which they can be used is given below

```
int write(int fd, const void *buffer, unsigned int
count);
int read(int fd, void *buffer, unsigned int count);
```

where

`buffer`: storage location for data
`count`: maximum number of bytes to be transferred
`fd`: file descriptor referring the open file for i/o operation

Figure 9.2 is a flow chart illustrating the copying of files from the source to the destination using direct I/O functions.

PROGRAM 9.2 illustrates the copy function in C. The source file (Fig. 9.2) is the file that is to be copied—it already exists. The destination file is the new file that will be created by the program after it performs the file copy function. If the program is not supplied with source and destination files, the program prompts the user with the `filecopy` format. The `open` and `create` function calls return an integer called the `file descriptor` which the program uses for referencing the files. The main program then calls the function `copy()` to read the data from the source file till the end of the file and keep writing the data read in each iteration to the destination file. The `copy` program copies not only files that have printable characters but also files with non-printable characters.

PROGRAM 9.1: FILECOPY.C

```
#include <stdio.h>
#include<fcntl.h>
#include <io.h>
char storage[1024];

main(argc,argv)
int argc;
char *argv[];
{
```

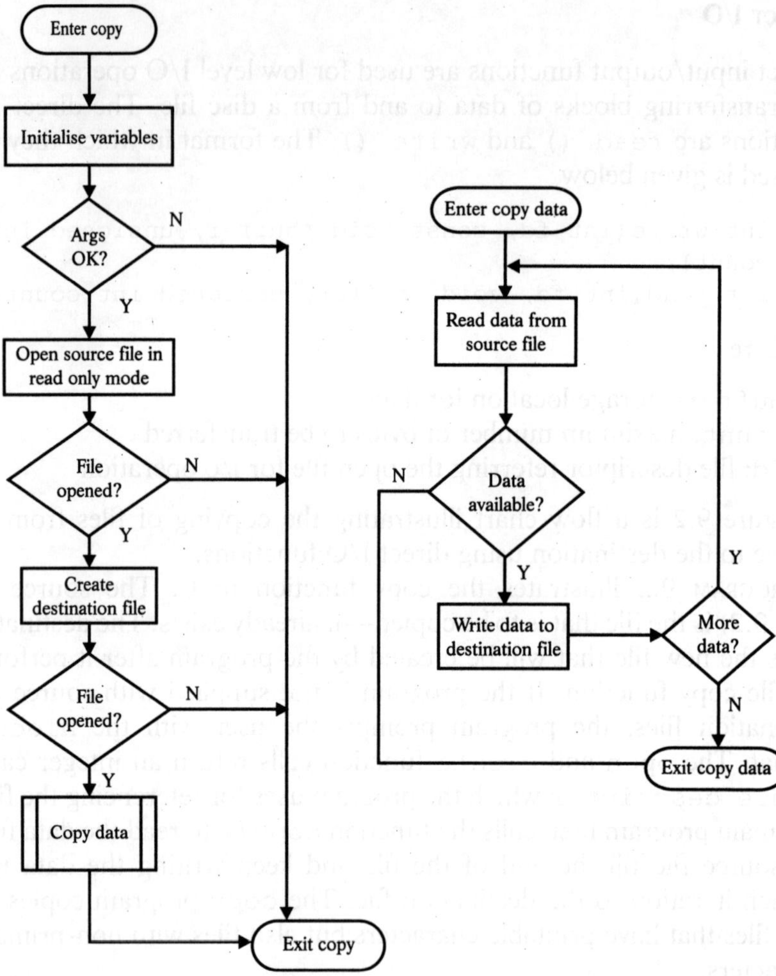

Fig. 9.2 Flow chart to copy files

```
/* file descriptors for source and destination files
*/
int fsource, fdest;

if(argc !=3)
{
  printf("\n Need source and destination files\n");
  printf("\n Format : filecopy <source>
<destination>\n");

  exit(1);
}
```

```
/* open the source file in read only mode */
fsource = open(argv[1],O_RDONLY);
if(fsource ==-1)
{
  printf("Cannot open source file %s\n", argv[1]);
  exit(1);
}

fdest = creat(argv[2],O_WRONLY);
if(fdest == -1)
{
  printf("Cannot open file %s\n", argv[1]);
  exit(1);
}

copyfiles (fsource,fdest);
printf("Source file %s is copied to destination file
%s\n",argv[1],argv[2]);
exit(0);
}

copyfiles(source, destination)
int source, destination;
{
int bytes_read;
while((bytes_read = read(source,storage,sizeof(stora
ge)))>0)
  write(destination,storage,bytes_read);
}
```

OUTPUT

RUN 1 filecopy

```
Need source and destination files

Format : filecopy <source> <destination>
```

RUN 2 filecopy seq.txt

```
Need source and destination files

Format : filecopy <source> <destination>
```

RUN 3 filecopy seq.txt seqnew.txt

```
Source file seq.txt is copied to destination file
seqnew.txt
```

File operations (i.e. format and character I/O operations) and some built-in functions can be used in bioinformatics to process DNA sequence files. PROGRAM 9.2 is an illustration of this. The program compares two consecutive patterns (each pattern has 10 nucleotides) within a given sequence. The sequence is taken from a `dna fasta file` '*`embl.fas`*'. After comparing two consecutive patterns, it will find and display the number of matches. The flow chart given in Fig. 9.3 describes the

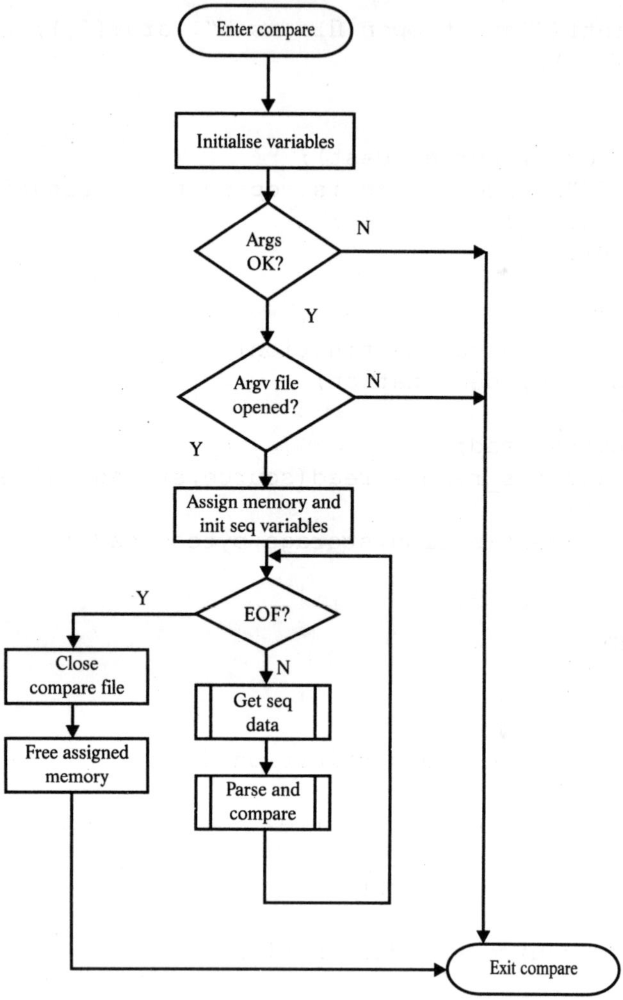

Fig. 9.3 Matching bases in consecutive patterns in a sequence file

---

[3] The sequences in the `embl.fas` file are listed in the Appendix.

operations involved in the program. One of the sequences used in the program, taken from the `embl.fas` file[3], is listed below:

```
Sequence 1

SQ Sequence 142 BP; 41 A; 32 C; 38 G; 31 T; 0 other;
agcagcagga agcactatgg gcgcagcgtc aataacgctg
acggtacagg ccagacaatt     60
attgtctggt atagtgcaac agcaaaacaa tttgctgagg
gctattgatg cgcaacagct     120
tctgttgcaa ctcacagtct gg  142
//
```

PROGRAM 9.2: COMPARE.C

```
#include <stdio.h>
#include <string.h>
#define MAX_ELEMENTS 20
#define TRUE 1
#define FALSE 0
struct seq {
  int no_seqs;
  int no_elements;
  int lineno;
  int match[MAX_ELEMENTS];
  int next_seq;
  };
struct seq *seq_p;

char* get_seq(char*,int,FILE*);
void parse_seq(char* seq);
int compare_nucleosides(char* token1,char* token2);
void init_seq_variables();
void print_seq();

main(argc,argv)
int argc;
char *argv[];
{
  char dna_seq[133],fname[20];
  char  *s;
  int i = 0;
  FILE *seq_fp;
```

```
if(argc <2)
{
      printf("Usage: compare <filename>\n");
      exit(0);
}
strcpy(fname,argv[1]);
printf("file name %s\n",fname);
if ( (seq_fp = fopen(fname,"r")) == NULL)
{
printf( "The file %s can not be opened\n",fname );
exit(0);
}
else {printf( "The file %s is opened\n",fname ); }

seq_p = (struct seq *) malloc(sizeof(struct seq));

if(seq_p==NULL)
{
      printf("\nNo memory available error\n");
      exit(0);
}
init_seq_variables();

/* Reads the sequence till the end of file, gets
each sequence terminated //
and parses each element in the sequence*/

while(!feof(seq_fp)) {
s = get_seq(dna_seq,132,seq_fp);
if(s == NULL)
{
      printf("\nEmpty file with no sequences\n");
      break;
}

/* Skips the first two lines in each sequence as
they have the header information */

if ( i++ < 2) continue;

/* If end of sequence is encountered, increment
the no of sequences by one */
if(strstr(dna_seq, "//"))
{
      i = 0;
      seq_p->no_seqs +=1;
```

```
        seq_p->lineno = 1;
        continue;
    }
    else {
        parse_seq(dna_seq);
        seq_p->next_seq=TRUE;
        seq_p->lineno +=1;

    }
  }
  fclose(seq_fp);
  free(seq_p);
  }

  void init_seq_variables()
  {
    seq_p->no_seqs = 0;
    seq_p->no_elements = 0;
    seq_p->next_seq = FALSE;
    seq_p->lineno = 1;
  }

  void parse_seq(char* seq)
  {
  char seps[]   = " \t\n";
  char *token,first_token[100];
  int res;
  static int idx;
  if(seq_p->next_seq)
  {
  idx = 0;
  seq_p->next_seq = FALSE;
  }
  /* Establishes string and get the first token: */
 token = strtok( seq, seps );
  seq_p->no_elements =0;

  while( token != NULL )
  {
  strcpy(first_token,token);
  /* While there are tokens in seq, get the next
  token: */
  token = strtok( NULL, seps );
  res = compare_nucleosides(first_token,token);
  if( res!=-1) {
```

```
    seq_p->match[idx++]=res;
    seq_p->no_elements +=1;
  }
  }
    print_seq();

  }
  void print_seq()
  {
  int j;
  printf("---------------------------------------\n");
  printf("\nSeqNo\t Lineno\t Fragment \t Match score
  \n");
  printf("---------------------------------------\n");

  for(j=0;j<seq_p->no_elements;j++)
  {
    printf("%d\t %d\t E%d - E%d \t   %d\n",seq_p->no_
  seqs,seq_p->lineno,j,j+1,seq_p->match[j]);
  }
  printf("\n\n");
  }

  int compare_nucleosides(char* token1,char* token2)
  {
    int match=0;

    if(strlen(token1) != strlen(token2)) return(-1);
    while(*token1 != '\0')
    {
          if( *token1++ == *token2++)
          {
          match+=1;
          }
    }
    return(match);
  }

  /*********************************************
  * read sequence data of length seq_len or till new
  line is encounterd.
  * Return the sequence data
  *********************************************/
```

```
char    *get_seq(seq, seq_len, seq_file)
char    *seq;
int     seq_len;
FILE    *seq_file;
{
  char *s;
  s = fgets(seq, seq_len, seq_file);
  if (s == NULL) return(NULL);
/*
  if (*seq == '>')
  {
  printf("Skip the sequence header\n");
  return(*seq);
  }
*/
return(seq);
}
```

OUTPUT

```
file name embl.fas
The file embl.fas is opened

-------------------------------------------------
SeqNo    Lineno       Fragment     Match score
-------------------------------------------------
0        1             E0 - E1          6
0        1             E1 - E2          0
0        1             E2 - E3          2
0        1             E3 - E4          2
0        1             E4 - E5          3

-------------------------------------------------
SeqNo    Lineno       Fragment     Match score
-------------------------------------------------
0        2             E0 - E1          4
0        2             E1 - E2          2
0        2             E2 - E3          0
0        2             E3 - E4          5
0        2             E4 - E5          1

-------------------------------------------------
```

```
SeqNo    Lineno      Fragment     Match score
---------------------------------------------
0        3           E0 - E1         1

---------------------------------------------
SeqNo    Lineno      Fragment     Match score
---------------------------------------------
1        1           E0 - E1         5
1        1           E1 - E2         0
1        1           E2 - E3         3
1        1           E3 - E4         1
1        1           E4 - E5         2

---------------------------------------------
SeqNo    Lineno      Fragment     Match score
---------------------------------------------
1        2           E0 - E1         4
1        2           E1 - E2         1
1        2           E2 - E3         0
1        2           E3 - E4         6
1        2           E4 - E5         1

---------------------------------------------
SeqNo    Lineno      Fragment     Match score
---------------------------------------------
1        3           E0 - E1         1
```

Chapter 10

Data Structures

STACK

A *stack* is an ordered collection of items in which insertions and deletions take place at the same end called the *top*. As there is only one opening where both insertions and deletions can take place it is a *last-in/first-out (LIFO)* structure. The open end of the stack as mentioned before is called the top. The store and retrieval operation of the stack are called *push* and *pop* respectively. The primitive operations performed on the stacks are

1. The item being pushed onto the stack
2. The item being popped from the stack

The data items in the stack are stored in consecutive order in the memory. The first item pushed onto the stack is said to be at the bottom of the stack. The item most recently pushed onto the stack is said to be on the top of the stack. A *stack pointer* (SP) contains the address of the top of the stack.

Figure 10.1 illustrates the operation of the stack. From the diagram, it is obvious that the bottom of the stack is at address X. The top of the stack is pointed to by the stack pointer and is at X+1 on the left side and at X+2 on the right side. The top of the stack changed from X+1 to X+2 as 200 was pushed on to the stack.

The scenarios shown in Fig. 10.2 explain the push and pop operations of the stack briefly.

The stack is initially empty as there are no items in it. Therefore, the top of the stack is –1. When 100 is pushed on to the stack, the top will be 1; and when 200 is pushed, the top will be 2.

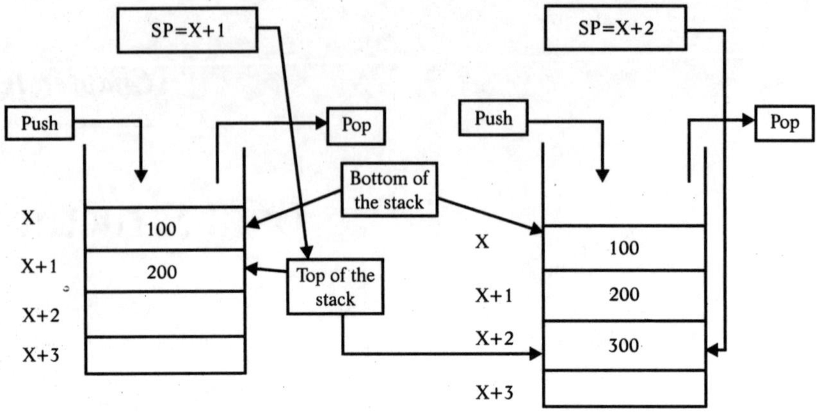

Fig. 10.1 Operation of the stack

The process is similar when an item is popped out of the stack except for the fact that the top will be decremented as opposed to the incrementing in case of push.

Let us see how mathematical expressions and their results are stored in a stack by the push and pop operations. Consider the postfix expression

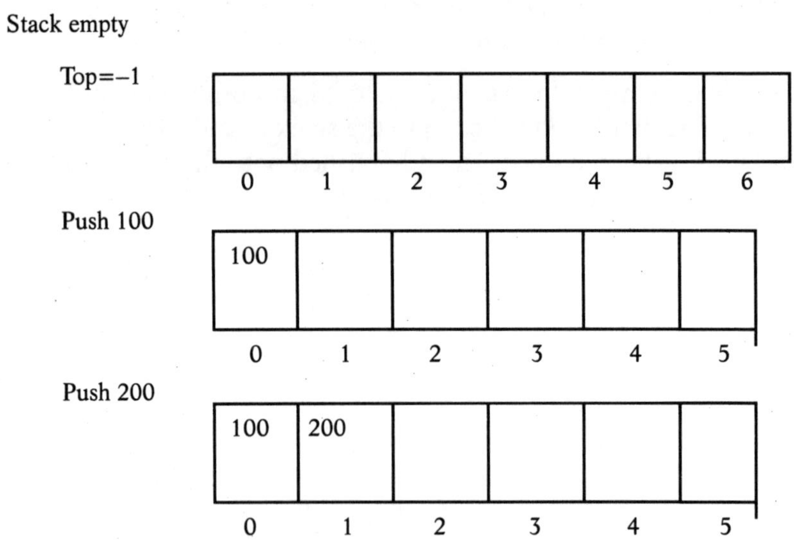

Fig. 10.2 Push operations in a stack

123*+.[1] The placement of the numbers in the stack is shown in columns 1, 2 and 3.

Multiplication operation * It is applied on two operands by popping. Top 2 and Top 1 are popped out and multiplied. The result is pushed back onto the stack which will be placed at Top = 1

Addition operation + Top 1 and Top 0 are popped out and added. The result is pushed back at Top 0.

Top = 0	1	1	1	1	7
Top = 1		2	2	6	
Top = 2			3		
operation				*	+

The program given below places a `fasta` sequence on the stack and creates a wordlist from it. The Smith–Waterman algorithm is used to create the wordlist. Different wordlists with the same wordsize can be created from the stack by modifying the print_WordList function or by manipulating the push and pop operations.

PROGRAM 10.1: STACK.C

```
/*
Creating a wordlist for a fasta sequence
*/
#include<stdio.h>
#define SEQLEN 12 /* Stack size for putting the
sequence in */
#define WordSize 6
typedef struct
{
 char seq[SEQLEN];
 int top;
} WordList;

void push(WordList *, char);
float pop(WordList *);
void init_WordList(WordList *);
int full(WordList *);
void print_WordList(WordList *);
void main()
{
```

[1] Postfix expressions are expressions where the operator appears after the operand.

```
char seq[SEQLEN] = {'g','c','t','g','g','a','a','g',
'g','c','a','t'};
char pop_base[7];
WordList fas;
int i;

init_WordList(&fas);

print_WordList(&fas);
printf("\nPush wordlist onto the stack\n");
for (i =0; i<SEQLEN;i++)
{
  push(&fas,seq[i]);
}

print_WordList(&fas);
for(i=0;i<WordSize;i++)
{
  pop_base[i] = pop(&fas);
}
pop_base[i] = '\0';

printf("\nWordlist popped out of the stack:\n ");
for(i=0;i<WordSize;i++)
{
  printf("%c %c",pop_base[i],0x20);
}
printf("\n");

print_WordList(&fas);

}

void push(WordList *f, char nt)
{
 f->seq[ f->top++ ] = nt;
}

float pop(WordList *f)
{
  (f->top)--;
  return (f->seq[f ->top]);
}

void init_WordList(WordList *f)
{
```

```
f->top = 0;
}

void print_WordList(WordList *f)
{
int i;
if (f->top == 0)
        printf("\nNo wordlist on the stack\n");
else
{
  printf("\nWordlist on the stack:\n ");
  for (i=0;i<f->top;i++)
  {
    printf("%c ",f->seq[i]);
  }
  printf("\n");
}
}
```

OUTPUT

```
No wordlist on the stack:

Push wordlist onto the stack

Wordlist on the stack:
g c t g g a a g g c a t

Wordlist popped out of the stack:
t a c g g a

Wordlist on the stack:
g c t g g a
```

QUEUE

A *queue* is a data structure that is marked with two open ends called the *front* and the *rear*. An element is inserted at the rear end and deleted from the front end (Fig. 10.3). Elements are removed in the same order they are stored. A queue operates on the principle of *first-in/first-out* (*FIFO*) or *first-come/first-served* (*FCFS*).

The primitive operations of a queue are

1. Adding an element to the queue: Insert operation
2. Deleting from the queue: Delete operation

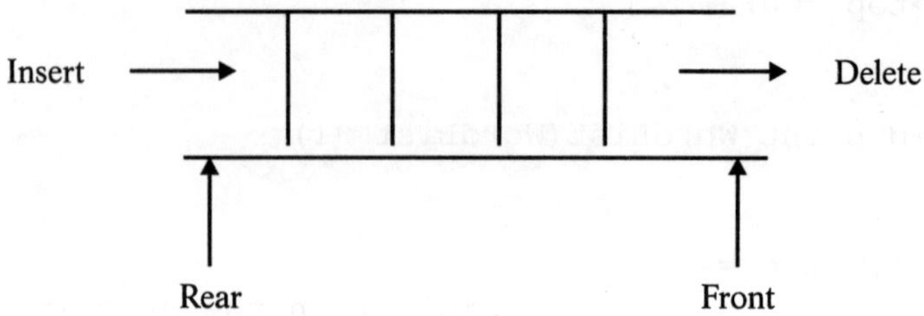

Fig. 10.3 Queue structure

A queue allows elements to be inserted and deleted from both ends. But the simplest queue is of the LIFO (last-in/first-out) type in which elements are added from one end and deleted from the same end (i.e. add-to-head implementation). A *circular queue* is a particular implementation of a queue where the insertion and deletion are totally independent. It has two indexes (i.e. pointers) called the *head* and the *tail* (Fig. 10.4). Memory storage in a circular queue is generally very efficient.

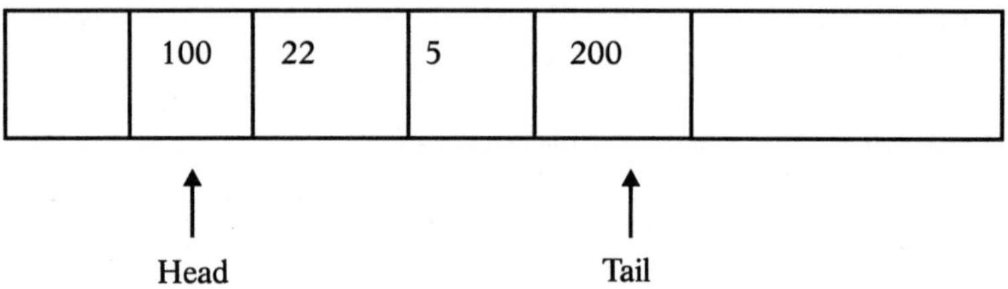

Fig. 10.4 Circular queue

To demonstrate the use of queues, let us create a program to build sequence frames from an ORF file containing the nucleoside sequences shown below

```
>gi|124376423|gb|BC132432.1| Mus musculus
carbonic anhydrase 1, mRNA (cDNA clone MGC:164063
IMAGE:40130709), complete cds
CCATGCATCTTCTCTGAAGCTAATCACAACCTAAATAAGAGAAAATAG
CAAGTGCAGACTGGGGATATGG
AAGCGAAAATGGTCCTGACCAATGGAGCAAGCTGTATCCCATTGCCAA
TGGAAACAACCAGTCTCCTATT
```

Each new sequence will start at a new line with a '>' to mark the beginning of the sequence. An ORF is a sequence within a messenger RNA that is bounded by a *start* and *stop* codon and which can be continuously translated. Each ORF has its own *start* and *stop* signals.

In our program where we build sequence frames from an ORF file, each frame built will have the structure shown in Fig. 10.5.

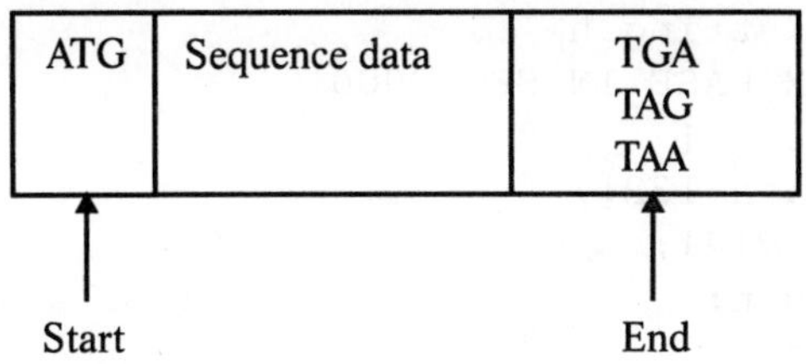

Fig. 10.5 ORF frame with begin and end patterns

All the frames that are built are put into a queue. Upon reaching the end of the ORF file, the frames will be printed from the queue and all the frames from the queue will be deleted. The flow chart to build the queue of frames is given in Fig. 10.6.

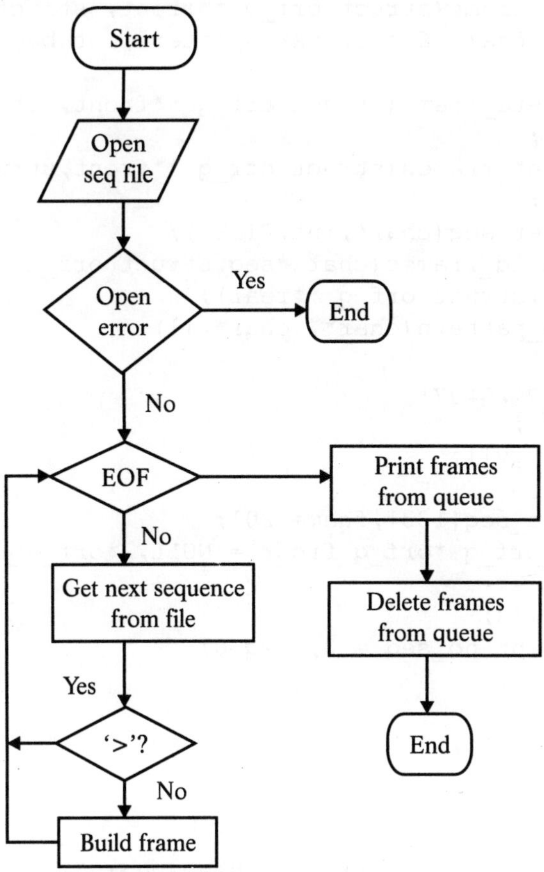

Fig. 10.6 Flow chart to queue frames

PROGRAM 10.2: ORF_QUE.C

```
#include <stdio.h>
#include <string.h>
#define MAX_BASE_IN_SEQ 2000
struct orf_q {
char fr_data[132];
char fr_end[4];
int fr_begin;
int fr_last;
int fr_seqno; /* seq number as in dna file */
int fr_number; /* frame number within a sequence */
struct orf_q *next;
};

static int no_frames = 0;
static int seqno;
int add_frame(struct orf_q **front, struct orf_q
**rear, char* frame,char* pattern,int begin,int
last);
int delete_frame(struct orf_q **front, struct orf_q
**rear);
int print_frames(struct orf_q **front,struct orf_q
**rear);
char* get_seq(char*,int,FILE*);
void build_frames(char *seq,struct orf_q
**front,struct orf_q **rear);
int find_pattern(char*, char* []);

main(argc,argv)
int argc;
char *argv[];
{
char dna_seq[133],fname[20];
struct orf_q *orf_q_front = NULL, *orf_q_rear =
NULL;
char    *s;
static int no_seq = 0,tseq=0;
int i,j=1;

FILE *seq_fp;
int counter;
if(argc <2)
{
  printf("Usage: orf_que <filename>\n");
  exit(0);
```

```
}
strcpy(fname,argv[1]);
printf("\nFile name: %s\n",fname);
if ((seq_fp = fopen(fname,"r")) == NULL)
{
  printf("\n The ORF file cannot be opened\n");
  printf("\n File Format: <xxxxxxxx.xxx> \n");

  exit(0);
}
else {printf("\n The ORF file %s is opened\n\
n",fname); }

while(!feof(seq_fp)) {
  s = get_seq(dna_seq,132,seq_fp);


  if(s == NULL)
  {
        break;
  }
  if(strchr(dna_seq, '>')) { ++tseq; continue;}
  else {
        ++no_seq;
        seqno = no_seq;
        build_frames(dna_seq,&orf_q_front,&orf_q_
rear);
  }
}

j = print_frames(&orf_q_front,&orf_q_rear);
if(j==0) printf("\n No more frames to print\n");

printf("\n  Partial sequence count : %2d\n",no_seq);
printf("\nTotal number of sequences : %2d\n",tseq);
for(i=0;i<no_seq;i++)
{
  j= delete_frame(&orf_q_front,&orf_q_rear);
  if(j==0){
        printf("\nNo more frames to delete\n");
        fclose(seq_fp);
        exit(0);
  }
}
return;
}
```

```
/*************************************************
* get_line reads an input line skipping blank and
comment lines
* seq parameter is not required. Define a string
array inside and use it
*************************************************/
char *get_seq(seq, seq_len, seq_file)
char *seq;
int seq_len;
FILE *seq_file;
{
char *s;

/* Read each line of input till end of file   */
s = fgets(seq, seq_len, seq_file);
if (s == NULL) return(NULL);
/* if (*s = EOF) return(char* (EOF));*/
if (*seq == '>')
{
 return(seq);  /* Read the sequence */
}
return(seq);
}
void build_frames(char *seq,struct orf_q
**front,struct orf_q **rear)
{
  char frame[132],fr_begin[] = "ATG";
  static char *fr_end[] = { "TGA","TAG","TAA"};
  char *begin_found = NULL,*end_found = NULL;
  int fr_begin_pos, fr_end_pos,j,idx;

memset(frame,'\0',131);
/* Locate the first occurrence of "ATG" in sequence.
If "ATG" is not found return from the function as
there is no begin frame in the sequence */
if ((begin_found = strstr(seq,fr_begin)) != NULL)
{
 /* Find the exact position of ATG in the sequence*/
       fr_begin_pos = (int) (begin_found - seq +1);

 /* Locate the first occurrence of the end frame in
the sequence */

strcpy(frame,begin_found+3);
idx = find_pattern(frame,fr_end);
```

```
/* If there is end pattern found, return from this
function */
  if (idx == -1) { return;}

/* Use the index and find the position of the end
frame in the sequence */

  if((end_found = strstr((begin_found+3),fr_
end[idx])) !=NULL)
  {
  fr_end_pos = (int) (end_found - (begin_found+3));

/* Now copy the frame between begin i.e. ATG and end
pattern. Decrease fr_end_pos as the count is from
zero and not from 1 */

        begin_found +=3;
for (j=0;j<(fr_end_pos);j++) /* end frame seq is
skipped */
  {
        frame[j] = *(begin_found++);
  }
        frame[j] = '\0';

/* Update orf_q data structure and queue orf data
along with frames */

  if((*frame)) {
  /* increment the value by one */
  ++no_frames;
  add_frame(front, rear,frame,fr_end[idx],fr_begin_
pos,fr_end_pos);
  }
return;
}

}
return;
}

/* Find the first pattern in the sequence and return
the frame. The patterns to be searched in the
sequence are "TGA","TAG","TAA". The begin frame from
pattern search for ATG in the sequence is passed as
the first argument and end patterns are passed as
second arg to the function below */
```

```
int find_pattern(char* begin, char* pattern[])
{
char *found=0, *end[3], fr[132];
int i, pos[3]={0,0,0},flag=0;
for(i = 0; i < 3; i++)
{
  memset(fr,'\0',131);
  found = strstr(begin,pattern[i]);
  if(found) {
    strcpy(fr,found);
    pos[i] = (int) (found-begin+1);
    if (pos[i] < 0) pos[i] =0;
    flag = 1;
    *found=0;
}

}
if(flag)
{
 if (pos[0])
 {
  if((!pos[1]) && (!pos[2])) return(0); /* first
pattern */
  if((!pos[1]) && (pos[2])) { return(pos[2] >
pos[0]) ? 0: 2;}
  if (pos[1] && pos[2])
  {
        return(pos[1] > pos[0]) ? 0:1;
  }
  if (pos[1])
  {
        if(!(pos[0]) && !(pos[2])) return (1);
        if(!(pos[0]) && (pos[2])) { return(pos[2] >
pos[1]) ? 1: 2;}
        if (pos[0] && pos[2])
        {
              return(pos[0] > pos[1]) ? 1:0;
        }
  }

  if (pos[2])
  {
        if(!(pos[0]) && !(pos[1])) return (2);
        if(!(pos[0]) && (pos[1])) { return(pos[1] >
pos[2]) ? 2: 1;}
```

```
        if (pos[0] && pos[1])
        {
              return(pos[0] > pos[2]) ? 2:0;
        }
}

}
  else return (-1);
}

/* Queue the frame (i.e. all nucleosides) between
ATG and the end pattern ("TGA","TAG","TAA"). All the
frames returned by build_frames are queued using
add_frame. On error returns a 0 and if successful
returns 1
*/

int add_frame(struct orf_q **front, struct orf_q
**rear, char* frame,char* pattern,int begin,int
last)
{
struct orf_q *temp;

temp = (struct orf_q *) malloc(sizeof(struct orf_
q));

if(temp==NULL)
{
  printf("\n No memory available error\n");
  return(0);
}

/* Get the partial sequence (frame data) and copy it
into fr_data */

strcpy(temp->fr_data,frame);
strcpy(temp->fr_end,pattern);
temp->fr_begin = begin;
temp->fr_last = last;
temp->fr_seqno = seqno;
temp->fr_number = no_frames;

temp->next = NULL;
if(*rear == NULL)
{
   *rear = temp;
```

```
   *front = *rear;
}
else
{
(*rear)->next = temp;
*rear = temp;
}
return(1);
}

/*
Deletes frames from the queue. If the queue is empty
returns a 0 and if successful returns 1
*/

int delete_frame(struct orf_q **front, struct orf_q
**rear)
{
struct orf_q *temp;
char* frame;
if((*front == *rear) && (*rear == NULL))
{
   printf(" \n The queue is empty\n");
   return (0);
}
temp = *front;
*front = (*front)->next;
if(*rear == temp) *rear = (*rear)->next;
free(temp);
return(1);
}

/*
Prints all frames from the queue or frames
selectively based on criteria. If the queue is
empty, returns a 0 and if successful returns 1.
Modify the program to print frame number and
sequence number
*/

int print_frames(struct orf_q **front,struct orf_q
**rear)
{
struct orf_q *temp,*restore;

if((*front == *rear) && (*rear == NULL))
```

```
{
   printf("\n The queue is empty\n");
   return(0);
}
restore = (*front);
temp = (*front);
printf("\nSeqno \tFrNum \t Find \t Begin \t End \t
Frame\n\n");
while(temp->next !=NULL) {

printf("%2d\t%2d\t%s\t%2d\t%2d\t%s\n",temp-
>fr_seqno,temp>fr_number,temp->fr_end,temp->fr_
begin,temp->fr_last,temp->fr_data);
  *front = (*front)->next;
   temp = (*front);
}
printf("%2d\t%2d\t%s\t%2d\t%2d\t%s\n",temp-
>fr_seqno,temp>fr_number,temp->fr_end,temp->fr_
begin,temp->fr_last,temp->fr_data);

(*front) = restore;
return(1);
}
```

OUTPUT

```
>orf_que dnaseq.fas
File Name: dnaseq.fas

The ORF File dnaseq.fas[1] is opened

Seqno FrNum Find  Begin  End  Frame

2       1    TGA    9     4    GTCC
3       2    TGA   26     9    ACTCCTCTC
6       3    TGA    5     4    GCTC
7       4    TGA   43    21    GCCTGGCAATCCTTGGCGTTT
8       5    TAA   42     3    CTC
10      6    TGA   28     6    AAAGTG
13      7    TAG    4    10    AGTCCTCAAT
19      8    TGA   10    46
   AGGAGGTGTCGCAACACCCCGTTCGCAATTGTCATTGCTCCGATCT
27      9    TGA    6    28
   AGGGCTTCACCAACTTGCTCTCCCAGAT
```

[1] Refer to Appendix to see all sequences in dnaseq.fas.

```
30      10     TGA      3      12   CCTTCCGTCTGC
34      11     TAG      8       2   CC
40      12     TGA     26      19   TCCTCGCTATTGCACATTG
45      13     TGA     22      33
   CGAATCGTCTGGCCTTGTGCGGGGCTTTCTACG
46      14     TAG     44      14   TCGCTATTCAAGTC
48      15     TAG     34      31
   AGCTGGGCTCTATGGTTCAGGGCCCTCAGGG
49      16     TAA     57       7   TGCCCGT
51      17     TAA     37      13   TGCTCGGGAACGT
52      18     TGA     12      16   GCGCCGTGCTGCGCGG
61      19     TGA     31      10   CGTTCGGCGT
63      20     TAA      9      17   GGCGCCCCAAACCTATT

Partial sequence count: 65

Total number of sequences: 3

The queue is empty

No more frames to delete
```

Linked List

A *linked list* is a collection of structures in which each structure contains at least one member whose value is the address of the next logically ordered structure in the list

In a list, items can be added and deleted at any location in the list whereas the same is not possible in an array as it has contiguous locations. The major advantages of the list are that

1. It removes the limitations of the array in terms of using only contiguous memory
2. The list can grow without any limitations

A list can also be defined as a collection of nodes (a node consists of all the data members of the structure and a pointer to the next item in the list). It has a head and a tail. The first node is always the head and the last is the tail. There are different types of lists:

1. Singly linked list
2. Doubly linked list
3. Circular list

Singly Linked List

A simple linked list of pH values is shown in Fig.10.7.

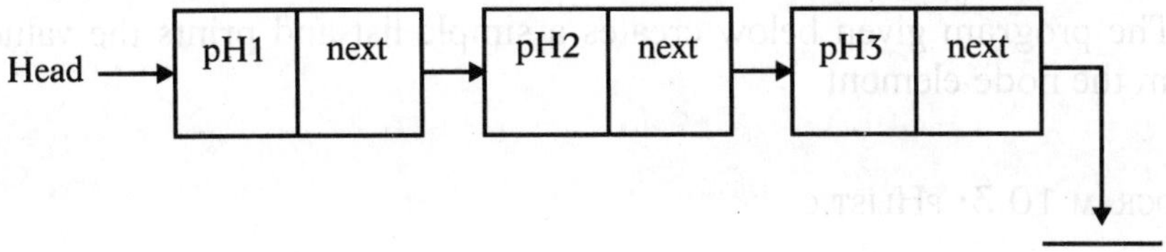

Fig. 10.7 A linked list of pH values

The node or list item `pH3` can be accessed by traversing the list using the next pointer. The following function helps access all the nodes in the list. It starts at the first node and accesses or displays the information of all the nodes until `NULL` is encountered.

```
display()
{
  temp = first;
while (temp != NULL)
{
  printf(" pH Value in the node is %d", temp->pH);
  temp = temp->next;
}
}
```

`first` and `temp` are pointers of type structure `pH` mentioned in PROGRAM 10.3.

Inserting a Node A new node item can be inserted anywhere in the list. The following algorithm inserts an element in a linked list.

1. Check if the list is empty.
2. If yes, then create memory for the node element and insert the node element in the first position.
3. If no, then move to the desired position and create memory to insert the node at that position.

In Fig. 10.8, `pH4` is inserted at the end of the list. The `next` of `pH3` will point to `pH4` and the `next` of `pH4` is set to NULL.

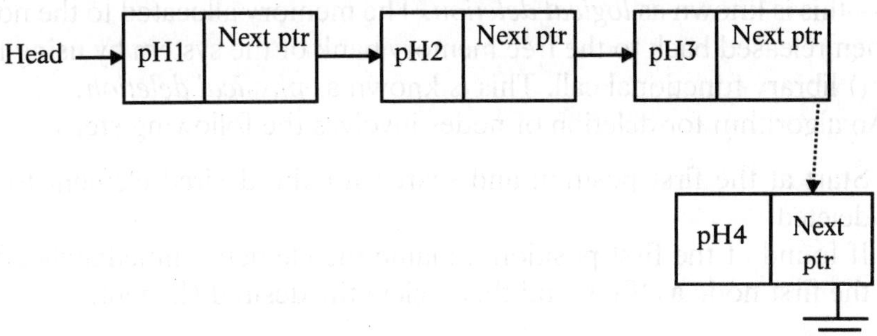

Fig. 10.8 Inserting pH4 into the list

The program given below creates a simple list and prints the values from the node element.

PROGRAM 10.3: PHLIST.C

```
#include <stdio.h>
struct pH{
int pH;
struct pH *next;
}

main()
{
struct pH pH1,pH2,pH3;
int pH1_next,pH2_next;

pH1.pH = 10;
pH2.pH = 5;
pH3.pH = 1;

pH1.next = &pH2;
pH2.next = &pH3;
pH3.next = NULL;

pH1_next = pH1.next->pH;
pH2_next = pH2.next->pH;

printf("pH2 = %d pH3 = %d\n",pH1_next,pH2_next);
}
```

OUTPUT

```
pH2 = 5 pH3 = 1
```

Deleting a Node The node to be deleted is first unlinked from the list—this is known as *logical deletion*. The memory allocated to the node is then released back to the free memory bank of the system by using the free() library functional call. This is known as *physical deletion*.

An algorithm for deletion of nodes involves the following steps.

1. Start at the first position and search for the desired element to be deleted.
2. If found at the first position, rename the element immediately after the first node as 'first' and then delete the desired element.

3. If the desired element is found after the first position in the list, the address part of the previous node is made to point to the address of the node next to the desired element; then the element is deleted.

CIRCULAR LIST

A circular list contains one node—usually the first one—called the *header* which finally points to itself i.e., the last node in the list will point to the header. Figure 10.9 shows an empty list. A list can be stated to be empty if it fulfills the following condition.

```
head->next == head
```

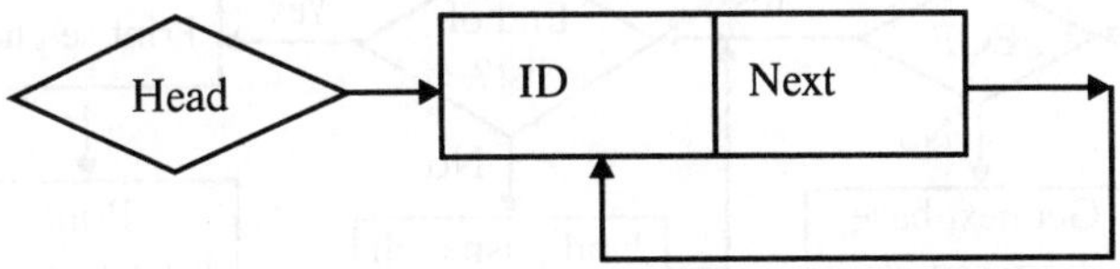

Fig. 10.9 Empty circular list

Figure 10.10 illustrates a circular list built from a DNA sequence file to find mismatch scores by comparing the sequences. This can then be displayed in a distance matrix[2]. The flow chart to generate the distance matrix is given in Fig.10.11.

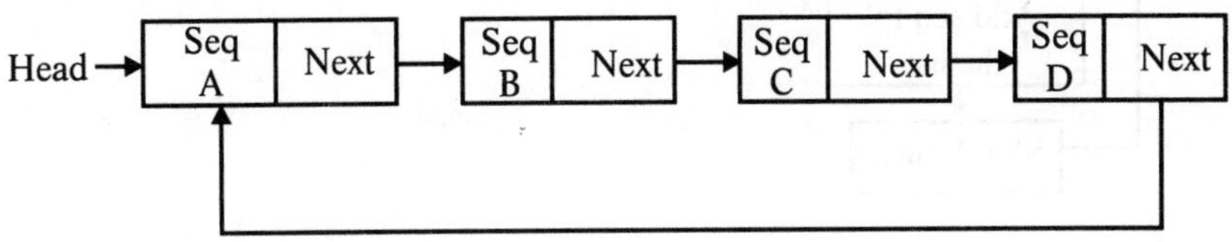

Fig. 10.10 Sequence list

PROGRAM 10.4 briefly explains the implementation of circular lists using sequences. It is assumed that the sequences in the input file are of the same length and contain only nucleotides a, t, g and c. However, the program only takes equal sequence lengths and ignores all the extra bases in the sequence during comparison. It is also assumed that each sequence is preceded by a header and terminated by '//'.

The mismatch scores for the sequence are stored in the global array instead of the `mm[]` array in the `seq` structure. The code for deleting the

---

[2] A matrix which displays the pairwise distances between two sequences is called a distance matrix.

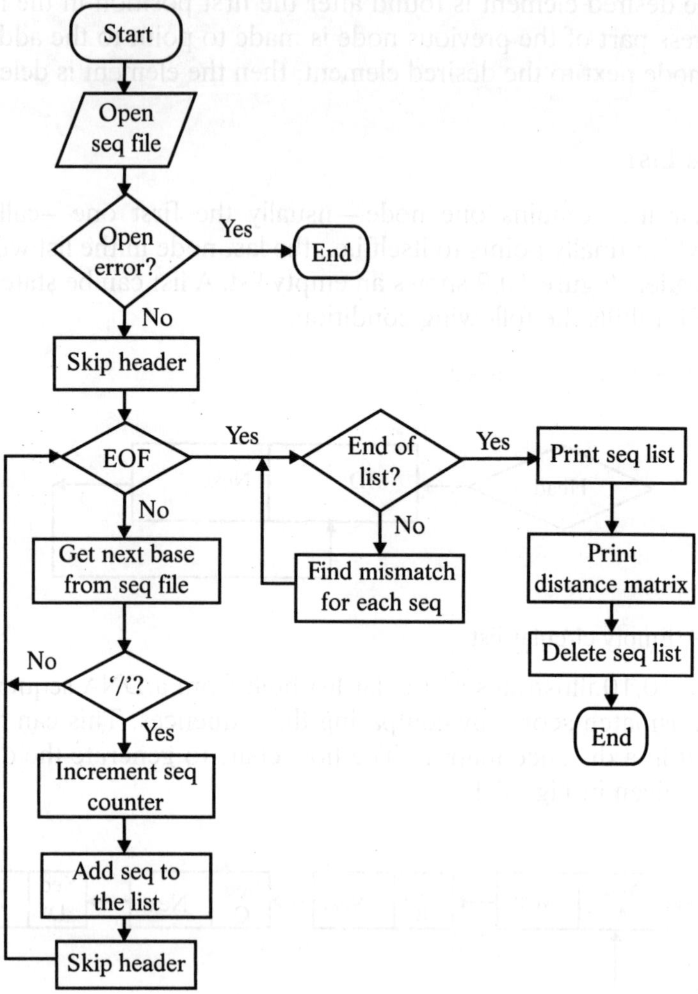

Fig. 10.11 Flow chart for generating a distance matrix

nodes in the list is not written and it is left to the reader to try our array structure and node deletion implementation.

PROGRAM 10.4: SEQLIST.C

```
#include <stdio.h>
#include <stdlib.h>
#define MAX_SEQ 4
#define SEQ_LEN 200
struct seq {
```

```
int mm[MAX_SEQ];
int seqid ;
char seq[SEQ_LEN]; /* place to hold the sequence
data */
struct seq *nextseq; /* link to the next element */
};

int mm[MAX_SEQ*4];
void init_seq_variables(struct seq *);
struct seq *addseq(struct seq *, char *);
void printseqlist (struct seq *);
int skip_header(char*, FILE*);
int mismatch(char*, char*);
void findscore (struct seq *,int);
struct seq *findseq(struct seq *, int);
void printscore();
void deleteseq();

int seqid = 65;
int no_of_seq = 0;

main(argc,argv)
int argc;
char *argv[];
{
char seq[200],fname[20],dnaseq[133];
char *atgc,base;
int res,count,i;
FILE *seq_fp;
struct seq *seqp = NULL,*temp=NULL;

if(argc <2)
{
  printf("Usage: seqlist <filename>\n");
  exit(0);
}
strcpy(fname,argv[1]);
printf("file name %s\n",fname);
if ((seq_fp = fopen(fname,"r")) == NULL)
{
  printf("The file %s cannot be opened\n",fname);
  exit(0);
}
else {printf("The file %s is opened\n",fname); }
```

```
/* Read the first two lines of the file and drop
them as they have header information which is not
required for comparison */

res = skip_header(dnaseq,seq_fp);
if(res == -1) exit(0);
memset(&seq,'\0',132);
atgc = &seq[0];

/* Read the sequence file till the end of file, get
sequence terminated by // and parse each element in
the sequence*/

while(!feof(seq_fp)) {

  base = getc(seq_fp);
  if(base == ' ' || base =='\n') continue;

/* If end of sequence is encountered, increment the
no of sequences by one */

  if(base == '/')
  {
        ++no_of_seq;
        seqp = addseq(seqp,&seq[0]);
        atgc = &seq[0];
        memset(&seq,'\0',132);
        res = skip_header(dnaseq,seq_fp);
        if(res == -1) break;

        continue;
  }
  *atgc++ = base;

}
fclose(seq_fp);
printf("\n The created list is given below.\n");
findscore(seqp,0);
count = seqp->seqid;
--no_of_seq;
for(i=1; i<no_of_seq; i++) {
  temp = findseq(seqp,count+i);
  findscore(temp,i);
}

/* Print the list */
```

```
printseqlist (seqp);

/* Print distance matrix for the sequences */
printscore();

/* Free all the elements from the list */
deleteseq();
}

int skip_header(char* dnaseq, FILE* seq_fp)
{
int i = 1;
char *s;
do
{
/* Read 80 characters or all characters until new
line which ever occurs first */
   s = fgets(dnaseq, 80, seq_fp);
         if(s == NULL)
   {
              return(-1);
   }
   if (strstr(s, "SQ") != NULL) i = 0;
} while (i>0);

}

struct seq *addseq(struct seq *seqp, char *atgc)
{
static int n = 0;
struct seq *temp;
if(seqp==NULL){
seqp=(struct seq*)malloc(sizeof(struct seq));

if(seqp==NULL) {
 printf("Error\n");
 exit(0);
 }
strcpy(seqp->seq,atgc);
 seqp->seqid = seqid++;
 seqp-> nextseq = seqp;
}
else
{
   temp = seqp;
   while (temp-> nextseq != seqp)
```

```
        temp = temp-> nextseq;
        temp-> nextseq = (struct seq*)malloc(size of
(struct seq));
        if(temp -> nextseq == NULL){
              printf("Memory Error\n");
        exit(0);
  }
  temp = temp-> nextseq;
  strcpy(temp->seq,atgc);
temp->seqid = seqid++;
  temp-> nextseq = seqp;
}

return (seqp);
}

void printseqlist (struct seq *seqp)
{
int i;
struct seq *temp;
temp = seqp;
printf("\nThe following sequences are used to find
scores: \n");
if(seqp!= NULL)
{
do
  {
  printf("\n%c\n",temp->seqid);
  printf("%s\n",temp->seq);
  printf("\n");
  temp=temp->nextseq;
  } while (temp!= seqp);
}
else
printf("The list is empty\n");
}

void findscore (struct seq *seqp,int idx)
{
struct seq *temp,*temp1;
char seqA[200], seqB[200];
int seqno[MAX_SEQ],i,score,row;

row = MAX_SEQ*idx+idx;
temp = seqp;
if(seqp!= NULL)
```

```
{

 strcpy(seqA,temp->seq);
 do
  {
        temp=temp->nextseq;
        strcpy(seqB,temp->seq);
        score = mismatch(seqA,seqB);
        mm[++row] = score;
  } while (temp->seqid != 'D');

}
else
printf("List empty - No score \n");
return;
}

struct seq *findseq(struct seq *temp, int id)
{
while(temp!=NULL)
  if(temp->seqid == id) return(temp);
  else temp = temp->nextseq;
return(0);
}

int mismatch(char* seqA, char* seqB)
{

char *a,*b;
int i,j,la,lb,score = 0;

a = seqA;
b = seqB;

la = strlen(a);
lb = strlen(b);

if(la == lb)
{
  j = la;
}
else
{
  j = ((la < lb) ? la:lb);
}
```

```
/* Add sequence validation logic as discussed in
dynamic programming to validate nucleotides in the
given sequence before calculating the score. No
validation logic is implemented in this program */

for(i=0;i<=j;i++) {
  if(isspace(*(a+i)) || isdigit(*(a+i))) continue;
  if(isspace(*(b+i)) || isdigit(*(b+i))) continue;
  if(*(a+i) != *(b+i)) score++;
}

return(score);
}

void printscore()
{
int i,j,count=0,base=65;
printf("\n \t \t A \t B \t C \t D \n\n");
for(i=0;i<(MAX_SEQ);i++)
{
  printf("%c\t",base+i);
  for(j=0;j<(MAX_SEQ);j++)
  {
        printf("\t %d ", mm[j+count]);
  }
  count +=j;
  printf("\n");
}
}
```

OUTPUT

f

RUN 1

```
>seqlist text.fas

file name text.fas
The file text.fas is opened
The created list is given below.

The following sequences are used to find scores:

Seq A
gtgctgcacg
```

```
Seq B
acgctgcacg

Seq C
gtgctgcacg

Seq D
gtatcacacg

          A     B     C     D

A         0     2     0     4
B         0     0     2     6
C         0     0     0     4
D         0     0     0     0
```

RUN 2

```
>seqlist embl.txt

File name embl.txt
The file embl.txt is opened
The created list is given below.

The following sequences are used to find scores:

Seq A
agcagcaggaagcactatgggcgcagcgtcaataacgctgacggtacagg
ccagacaatt60
attgtctggtatagtgcaacagcaaaacaatttgctgagggctattgatg
cgcaacagct120
tctgttgcaactcacagtctgg142

Seq B
gcagcaggaagcactatgggcgcagcgtcaataacgctgacggtacagg
ccaaacaaata60
ttgtctggtatagtgaatcagccaaacaatttgctgagggctattgagg
cgcaacatatt120
ctgttgcaactcacagtctgg141

Seq C
attgtctggtatagtgcaacagcaaaacaatttgctgagggctattgat
gcgcaacagct120

Seq D
gcagcaggaagcactatgggcgcagcgtcaataacgctgacggtacagg
ccaaacaaata60
ttgtctggtatagtgaatcagccaaacaatttgctgagggctattgagg
cgcaacatatt120
```

	A	B	C	D
A	0	111	43	94
B	0	0	47	1
C	0	0	0	47
D	0	0	0	0

DOUBLY LINKED LISTS

Doubly linked lists are like singly linked lists, except that each node has two pointers—one to the next node, and one to the previous node (Fig.10.12). The doubly linked list is more flexible and has the following advantages:

1. It is possible to traverse the list both forward and backward.
2. Insertion of nodes anywhere—before a node, after a node, at the front of the list, and at the end of the list—is easy.
3. Deletion of nodes is easy.

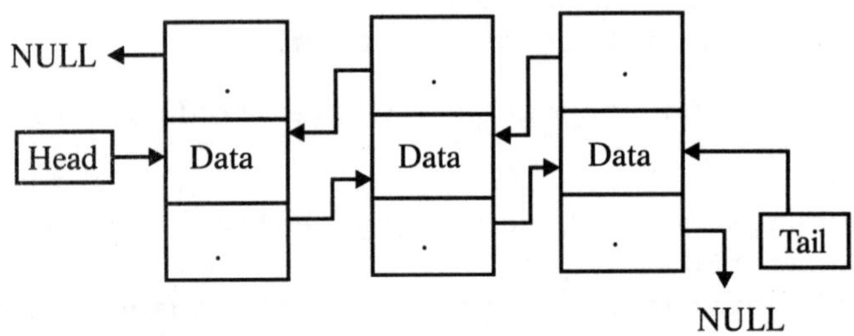

Fig. 10.12 Doubly linked list

The functions AddHead() and RemoveNode() create a sequence list and remove a node from the list respectively. The format for these two functions is given below.

```
struct seqList
{
struct seqNode * head, * tail;
};

struct seqNode
{
struct seqNode * next, * prev;
};

void AddHead (struct seqList * list, struct seqNode
* node)
```

```
{
node->next = list->head;
node->prev = (struct seqNode *)&(list->head);
list->head->prev = node;
list->head = node;
}

void RemoveNode (struct seqNode * node)
{
node->prev->next = node->next;
node->next->prev = node->prev;
}
```

TREE

The data structures that have been discussed so far, like stacks and queues, are linear data structures. Non-linear data structures help in situations where members may have multiple successors. For example, a parent may have two or more children. A *tree* is a non-linear data structure which is encountered frequently in everyday life. In a linked structure, each node has a link which points to the next node whereas in a tree structure, each node points to several other nodes. A tree structure is considered to be a powerful data structure that can be employed in a variety of applications.

It contains a set of nodes starting from the *root* node. The first node is always called the root node. A given node in the tree which is called the *parent* may have zero or more nodes which are called *children.* The children of the same parent are called *twins* (logical). Trees are *hierarchical* data structures representing a relationship between a parent and a child data item. Tree may be *balanced* (i.e. each parent has equal number of children) or *unbalanced*.

In Fig.10.13 RNA is the root node and mRNA is the child of CRNA while tRNA and rRNA are children of NCRNA, which in turn, have children called *descendents*. Leaf nodes in a tree do not have children. 50S, 30S, 60S and 40S are leaf nodes.

A tree can have many sub-trees. A sub-tree is nothing but a node and all its descendents (Fig.10.14).

The number of nodes on the longest path from root to leaf is called the *height of the tree*. In Fig.10.14 the height of the tree is 3. Figures 10.15–10.16 give more illustrations of how the tree height is calculated.

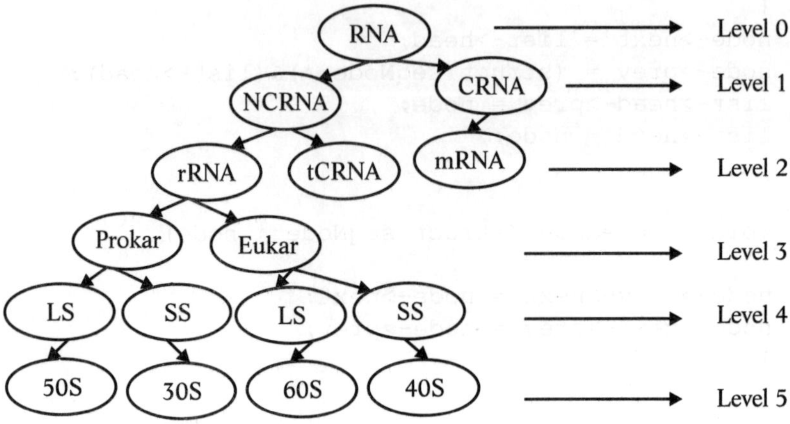

RNA: Ribonucleic acid; tRNA: Transfer ribonucleic acid; mRNA: messenger ribonucleic acid; rRNA: Ribosomal ribonucleic acid; NCRNA: Non-coding RNA; CRNA: Coding RNA; SS: Small sub-unit; LS: Large sub-unit

Fig. 10.13 RNA: Classification of genes in a tree with node levels

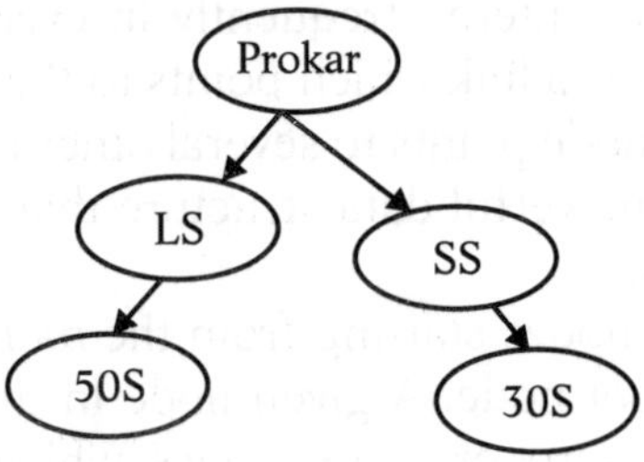

Fig.10.14 A sub-tree

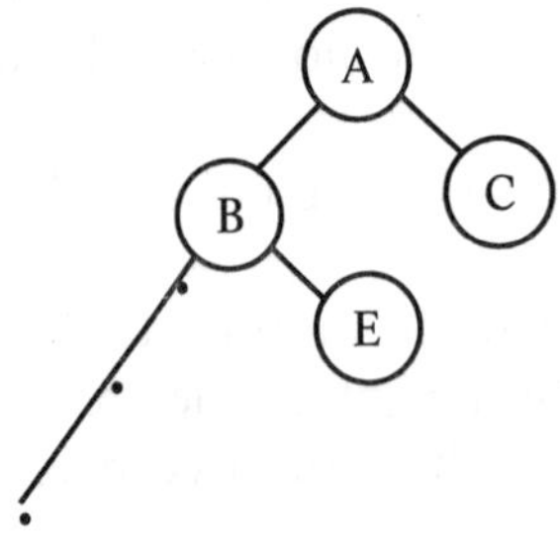

Fig.10.15 Height of the tree is 5

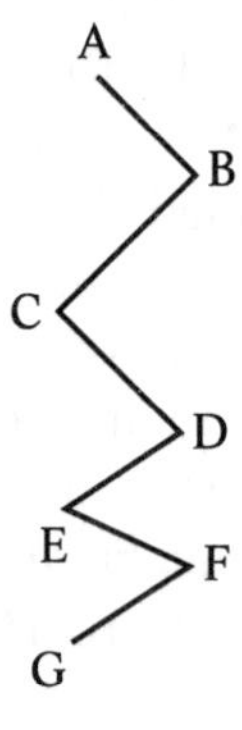

Fig.10.16 Height of the tree is 7

BINARY TREE

The simplest form of a tree is a binary tree. The *binary tree* is a balanced tree where each parent has two children—a parent node cannot have more than two children. It has a root node like other trees and left and right sub-trees called the *left child* and the *right child* respectively. Each child is again a binary tree. It takes lesser time to access nodes in binary trees as the number of children is limited unlike in a general tree. The nodes at the lowest levels of the tree (the ones with no sub-trees) are called *leaves* similar to a general tree. Figure 10.17 shows a simple biological binary tree.

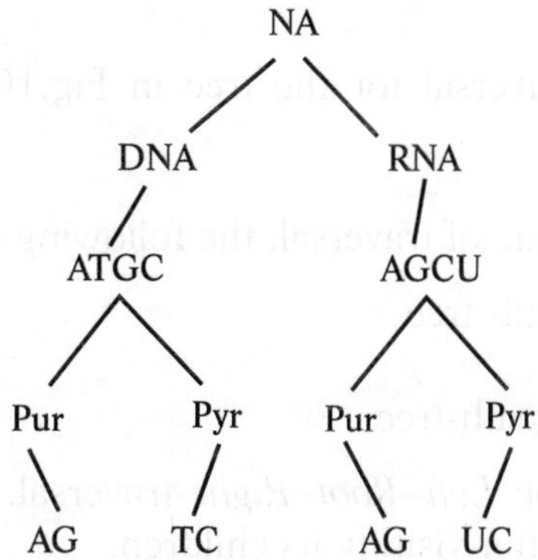

Fig.10.17 Biological binary tree

TREE TRAVERSAL

A binary tree can be traversed in three different ways.

1. Pre-order
2. Post-order
3. In-order

We will use the binary tree in Fig.10.18 to illustrate the different ways in which a tree can be traversed.

Pre-order In this traversal, the root is visited first, followed by a traverse to the left sub-tree and then to the right sub-tree. It is also called the *Root–Left–Right* traversal.

The pre-order traversal for the tree in Fig.10.18 is '– + a * b c * d e'.

Post-order In this traversal, the left sub-tree should be visited first, followed by traversal to the right and then the root. Therefore, it is also called the *Left–Right–Root* traversal.

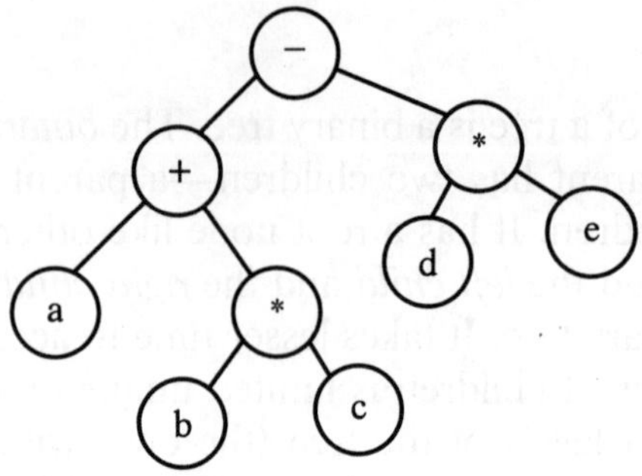

Fig.10.18 Illustration of tree traversal

The post-order traversal for the tree in Fig.10.18 is 'a b c * + d e * –'.

In-order In this mode of traversal, the following steps are followed.

1. Traverse the left sub-tree
2. Visit the root
3. Traverse the right sub-tree

It is also called the *Left–Root–Right* traversal. To explore the tree, each node is visited after visiting its children.

The pseudo algorithm[3] for in-order traversal is given below.

```
Begin
  if root is nil, then return
  Inorder (T->Left): traverse the left sub-tree
recursively
  visit (T): Visit the tree root
  Inorder (T->Right): traverse the right sub-tree
recursively
End
```

Using the in-order traversal algorithm, let us traverse the tree in Fig. 10.18.

STEP 1

The root of the tree is '–' and therefore it is not null.

---

[3] Pseudo algorithms are natural language programs modelled to look like statements available in many programming languages.

STEP 2

Traverse the left sub-tree recursively means that:

The root of the tree is now '+'; traverse its sub-tree and the root of the new tree is 'a'.

STEP 3

As there are no more sub-trees to the left of 'a', visit the parent of 'a' or its root which is '+'.

STEP 4

Now traverse to the right sub-tree of '+' and traverse the right sub-tree recursively. Use the same strategy for the right sub-tree as mentioned in STEP 2 and STEP 3.

Therefore, the in-order traversal of the tree in Fig.10.18 is a + b * c – d * e.

ARRAY BASED BINARY TREE

Binary trees can be stored and arranged linearly in an array which is a sequential and consecutive list of elements. The arrangement is based on the node levels in the tree. All nodes found at a particular level are placed consecutively one after the other in the array. Let us consider the tree shown in Fig.10.19. Each node is found at a particular level—level of a node is the length of the path from the root to the node. In the figure, Glyceral is at 0 level; Erythrose and Threose are found at level 2 and so on. We will now try to map this tree into an array.

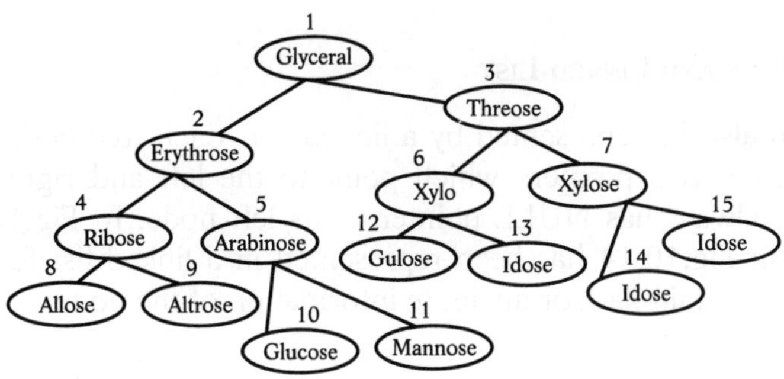

Fig.10.19 Classification of carbohydrates: Tree for array conversion

Mapping Let us say the array is called `name[10]`[4]. `name[0]` has the root element Glyceral. The next level children are mapped into the next consecutive locations of the array i.e. name[1] and name[2] and so on with all other elements in different levels of the tree. Therefore, the array will be as in Table 10.1.

Element	Glyceral	Erythrose	Threose	Ribose	Arabinose	Xylose	Xylo	Allose	Altrose	Glucose
Index	0	1	2	3	4	5	6	7	8	9

Table 10.1 Array of tree elements

We can also list out the index of a node along with the index of its children as given in Table 10.2.

Index	Node	Left child index	Right child index	
0	Glyceral	2	3	Root
1	Erythrose	4	5	
2	Threose	6	7	
3	Ribose	8	9	
4	Arabinose	10	11	
5	Xylose	12	13	
6	Xylo	14	15	
7	Allose	–1	–1	
8	Altrose	–1	–1	
9	Glucose	–1	–1	
10	Mannose	–1	–1	

Table 10.2 Index of nodes along with their children

BINARY TREE AND LINKED LIST

Trees can also be represented by a linked list. Each tree node contains besides data, two pointers which point to the left and right node. A leaf node always has NULL pointer as its left node. In Fig.10.19, the sub-tree in Fig.10.14 has been represented in a linked list form. Each node may contain data or attribute information of the node.

---

[4] The figure '10' in the square brackets refers to the number of elements in the array (for further details, refer to Chapter 6). Therefore, name[2] of name[10] would refer to the 2nd element in the array. The number 2 is the index of the 2nd element.

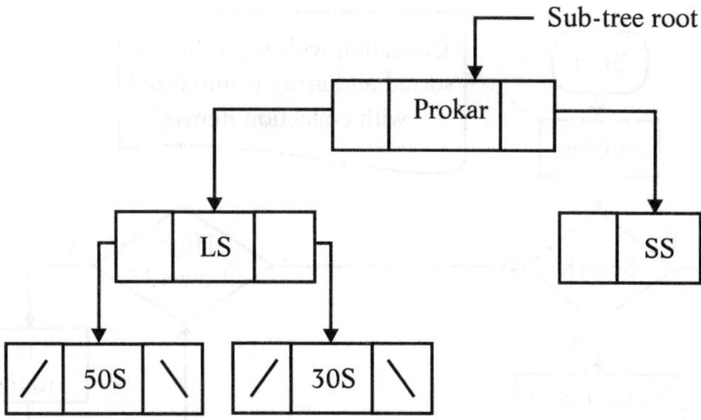

Fig.10.20 Linked representation of a tree

BINARY SEARCH

Binary search is an important operation on data structures. It involves searching for a desired element by repeatedly dividing a sorted list or array in half.

Let us assume that we have a collection of items. This collection of items is sorted in either descending or ascending order and put into an array. In binary search, the key value or the desired value is compared with the item in the middle position of the array. If there is a match, the item is returned immediately. If the key value is less than the value of the middle item, then the item that is to searched for must lie in the lower half of the array; if it is greater, than the desired item must lie in the upper half of the array. So the search procedure is repeated on the lower (or upper) half of the array till the item is found. The flow chart of binary search is given in Fig.10.21.

Binary search is recursive in terms of determining whether the search key lies in the lower or upper half of the array. If in the program (high – low < 2) or low > high then it is obvious that there are no elements to search for in the partition and therefore the program returns the statement that no match was found. If an element with a matching key value is found, it will be returned and the program will end.

Let us apply binary search to the pH table of values given below to find whether pH 8 is present in the table.

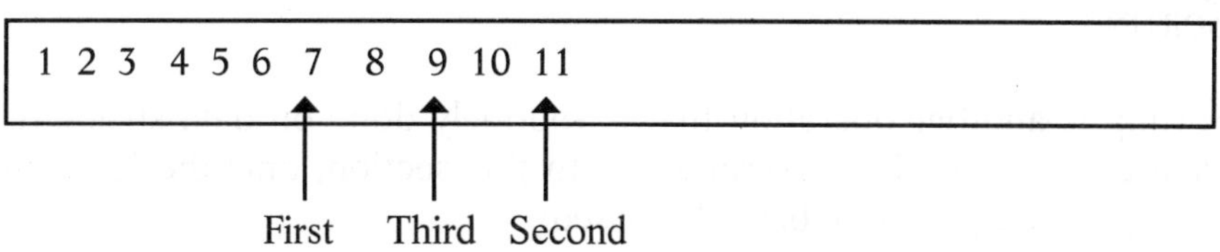

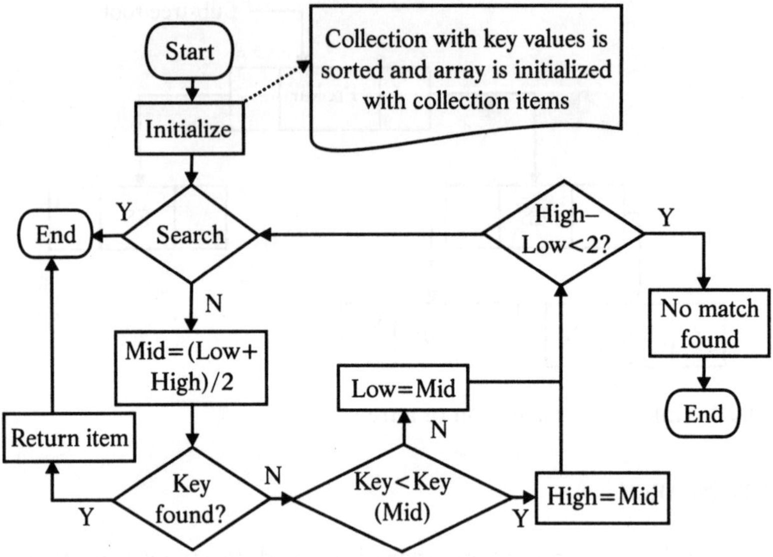

Fig.10.21 Binary search flow chart

In the first pass,

High = 11 and Low = 0; therefore, Mid = 11/2 = 6 (decimal rounded to higher value)
Value to search = 8
Value at Mid = 6
Therefore, key value to be searched is greater than the key value at Mid.

In the second pass,

Low = 6, High = 11 and then Mid = (11+6)/2 which is 9 (rounded)
The value is higher than the value to be searched.

In the third pass, find again the mid value

Low = 6; High = 9 and Mid = (9+6)/2 = 8
We could find the search value in a table of values after 3 passes.

In a similar way, we can apply binary search to a table of strings and search for a desired string.

SORTING

Sorting is another operation that is routinely done on data structures. Data can be sorted in several ways. In this section, only the following sorting techniques have been discussed:

1. Selection sort
2. Bubble sort

SELECTION SORT

This technique involves a selective interchange of the smallest data element with the element at a given position. The basis of selection sort as well as bubble sort is interchange of two data elements. The two data elements are swapped using a temporary storage area as shown in Fig.10.22.

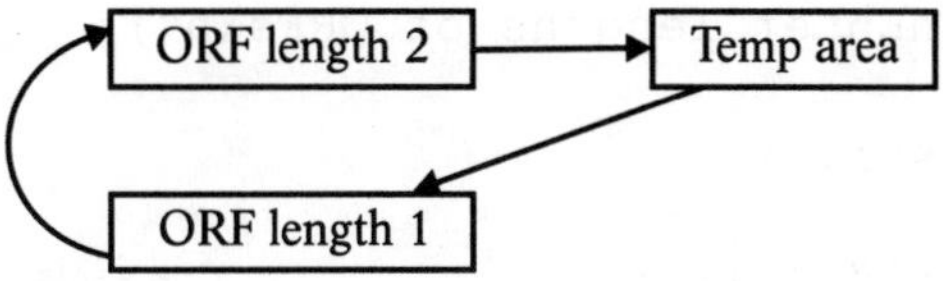

Fig.10.22 Swapping of data elements

In a collection of data elements that are to be sorted either in ascending or descending order, first a search for the smallest elements is made and this element is swapped with the first element. From this it is clear that the collection of *N* elements cannot be sorted in one pass or go, but goes through *N*–1 passes. Let us illustrate selection sort with an example. Assume that array S has five data elements—44, 33, 55, 22 and 11—and it is unsorted. The number of passes that the array has to undergo is shown in Fig.10.23.

44	33	55	22	11	Pass 1: Select 11 Swap 11 with S[0]
11	33	55	22	44	Pass 2: Select 22 Swap 22 with S[1]
11	22	55	33	44	Pass 3: Select 33 Swap 33 with S[2]
11	22	33	55	44	Pass 4: Select 44 Swap 44 with S[3]
11	22	33	44	55	Final sorted array S

Fig.10.23 Number of passes in selection sort

The program given below sorts ORF (open reading frame) lengths for a given number of ORFs using selection sort.

PROGRAM 10.5: SELSORT.C

```
#include <stdio.h>
main()
{
int i,j,temp,N,s[100];
printf("\nEnter the number of ORFs to sort \n");
scanf("%d",&N);
printf("\nEnter lengths of ORFs\n");

for(i=0;i<N;i++)
{
  scanf("%d",&s[i]);
}

for(i=0;i<N;i++)
{
  for(j=0;j<N;j++)
   {
  if(s[i]<s[j])
   {
     temp = s[i];
     s[i] = s[j];
     s[j]=temp;
         }
   }
}
printf("\nThe sorted ORF lengths are \n");
for(i=0;i<N;i++)
{
  printf("%5d",s[i]);
}
}
```

OUTPUT

```
Enter the number of ORFs to sort
5

Enter lengths of ORFs
44
33
55
```

```
22
11

The sorted ORF lengths are
11 22 33 44 55
```

BUBBLE SORT

A bubble sort algorithm involves comparing adjacent data elements. It interchanges or swaps the elements if necessary and repeats the comparison pass until no swaps need to be done.

In the first pass, the first element is compared with the second and the second with the third and so on until the last but one element ($N - 1$) is compared with the last element (N). If the second element is smaller than the first, the elements are interchanged; otherwise it is assumed that the elements are in sorted order and passed with no interchange.

In bubble sort, it is evident that there are $N - 1$ passes for N data elements. In the first pass, $N - 1$ pairs of elements are compared and the smallest element is moved to the smallest array position at the end of the pass. The same is done for all other passes except that the second has $N - 2$ pairs of element and third pass has $N - 3$ pairs of elements and so on (Fig. 10.24).

The program given below sorts ORF (open reading frame) lengths for a given number of ORFs using bubble sort.

PROGRAM 10.6: BUBSORT.C

```
#include <stdio.h>
main()
{
int i,j,temp,N,pairs,s[100];
printf("\nEnter the number of ORFs to sort \n");
scanf("%d",&N);
printf("\nEnter lengths of ORFs\n");
for(i=0;i<N;i++)
{
  scanf("%d",&s[i]);
}
pairs = N-1;
for(i=0;i<N-1;i++)
{
     for(j=0;j<=pairs-i;j++)
      {
          if(s[j+1]<s[j])
```

First iteration of bubble sort

44	33	55	22	11	Interchange 44 and 33
33	44	55	22	11	No interchange
33	44	22	55	11	Interchange 55 and 22
33	44	22	11	55	Interchange 55 and 11

Second iteration of bubble sort

33	44	22	55	11	Interchange 44 and 22
33	22	44	11	55	Interchange 44 and 11
33	22	11	44	55	Interchange 44 and 11

Third iteration of bubble sort

33	22	11	44	55	Interchange 22 and 33
22	33	11	44	55	Interchange 33 and 11
22	11	33	44	55	Interchange 33 and 11

Fourth iteration of bubble sort

22	11	33	44	55	Interchange 22 and 11
11	22	33	44	55	Final sorted array

Fig.10.24 Number of passes in bubble sort

```
      {
         temp = s[j];
             s[j] = s[j+1];
            s[j+1]=temp;
            }
         }
```

```
}
printf("\nThe sorted ORF lengths are \n");
for(i=0;i<N;i++)
{
  printf("%5d",s[i]);
}
}
```

OUTPUT

```
Enter the number of ORFs to sort
5

Enter lengths of ORFs
44
33
55
22
11

The sorted ORF lengths are
11 22 33 44 55
```

Chapter 11

Case Studies

MATRIX MEMORY MANAGEMENT

Two-dimensional arrays and matrices have very important applications in bioinformatics. We have already discussed arrays in Chapter 6, but in this section we will get into more detail about how the information in a matrix is stored. This becomes important as students in bioinformatics need to know how to access matrices efficiently.

Figure 11.1 briefly explains how row mapping is used to store in memory, the data contained in a matrix along with its pointer onto a two-dimensional array. The pointer `sp`, is actually a pointer to an array of *y pointers*, of type `int` in case of dynamic programming. Each pointer in the array of pointers points to an array of *x data elements.* Higher dimensional arrays can be declared in a similar way with more layers of pointers.

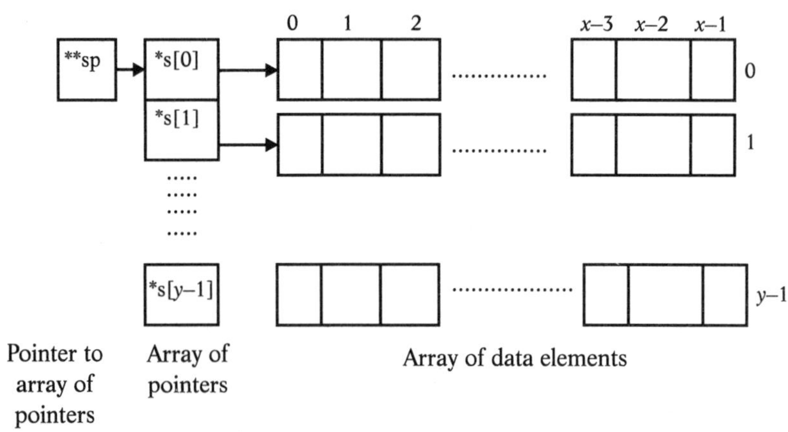

Fig.11.1 Pointer based multi-dimensional array structure

We will explain the above storage of two-dimensional arrays using an example. Let us say s_{ij} is a 3 × 4 matrix (Fig.11.2) filled with integer values. The matrix can be accessed using two kinds of arrays namely the index array and the value array. Figure 11.3 shows the index array which is nothing but the array of integer pointers (`s[0]` of type `int`) referenced by s and of type integer.

$$\begin{pmatrix} s00 & s01 & s02 & s03 \\ s10 & s11 & s12 & s13 \\ s20 & s21 & s22 & s23 \end{pmatrix}$$

Fig.11.2 Matrix s_{ij}

int **s ⟶

s0	s1	s2

Fig.11.3 Index array

It is called an *index array* because all the pointers in it serve as an index to access individual arrays with values. An array of all the elements of the matrix is called a *value array*. In our example, all the elements of type integer in s_{ij} constitute the value array. The size of the value array is *row length* × *column length*. Matrix s_{ij} (Fig. 11.2) has 3 rows and 4 columns. Therefore, a row-mapped[1] value array of the matrix has 3 × 4 = 12 elements of type integer (Fig.11.4).

s00	s01	s02	s03	s10	s11	s12	s13	s20	s21	s22	s23

Fig.11.4 Value array

STEPS FOR OPERATION

1. Instantiate the index array (array length = row length)
2. Instantiate the value array (array length = row length × column length)
3. Use index array pointers to access each row by pointing to the beginning of each row in the matrix as mentioned below.

---

[1] Row mapping has already been discussed in Chapter 6.

```
for(i=1;i<row length; i++)
    s[i] = s[i-1]+column length;
```

For s_{ij}, the index array length = 3 and value array length = 12. Therefore, if we need to access the elements of the first row, i = 1; s[1] = s[0]+4; the pointer has to be positioned at s10.

DYNAMIC PROGRAMMING

Dynamic programming is an efficient programming technique for solving certain combinatorial problems. It is particularly important in bioinformatics as it is the basis of sequence alignment algorithms for comparing protein and DNA sequences. Comparing of sequences, gene recognition, prediction of RNA structures and hundreds of other problems are solved nowadays by developing variations of dynamic programming.

ROLE OF DYNAMIC PROGRAMMING IN BIOINFORMATICS

Dynamic programming can be applied to great advantage in problems where inputting data results in an extensive search for optimal solutions to a number of smaller problems (sub-problems). If the solutions to sub-problems are shared and the principle of sub-problem optimality holds, dynamic programming can evaluate such a search in minimal time. Therefore, they are used extensively in computational molecular biology. Determination of sequence data (information about the nucleic acids and proteins in a sequence) are done on an industrial scale today. Dynamic programming helps to give meaning to these molecular data.

It can be used to assemble DNA sequence data from fragments that are delivered by automated sequencing machines, and to determine the intron/exon structure of eukaryotic genes. Dynamic programming can be used to infer the function of proteins by comparing it to other similar proteins with known functions. It is used to predict the secondary structure of functional RNA genes or regulatory elements. The first use of the dynamic programming approach for the alignment of biological sequences was reported by Saul Needleman and Christian Wunsch in 1970 (Needleman, S.B and C.D. Wunsch. 1970. *J.Mol.Biol.* 48:443–453) and later in a slightly modified form by Sellers (Sellers, P.H. 1974. *SIAM J.Appl.Math.* 26:787).

Let us try to solve the alignment problem—the best way two sequences can be aligned. Dynamic programming requires us to divide the problem into smaller sub-problems and optimally solve them one by one. The smallest unit that the alignment problem can be sub-divided into is the comparison of amino acid pairs.

The best alignment for two sequences can be determined using a two-dimensional array. Let each dimension represent one sequence. The optimal alignment can then be drawn as a path originating at either border from one sequence and ending at the opposing border for the other sequence—all cells traversed by this path are aligned sequence pairs.

Permissible paths in this process are all that would extend the alignment. Thus in the sample matrix below, the cells that can be reached from the cell (E,M) marked with an X, are indicated with a cross. To align with a cell in the diagonal means an alignment in the next position. To align with an off-diagonal cell requires the insertion of a corresponding number of gaps.

```
    A B C D E F G H I J
  +--------------------
K |
L |
M |         X
N |           + + + + +
O |           +
P |           +
Q |           +
R |           +
S |           +
```

The idea that Needleman and Wunsch had is explained below.

Let us compute for every cell the highest possible score that can be obtained for a path originating from that cell. That is simply done by looking in all the elements permissible for extending the path, and adding the highest value found to the contents of the cell. If this is done in an orderly way (Fig.11.5), the highest score found is the global maximum alignment score. The program given below provides an optimal solution for the alignment problem.

PROGRAM 11.1: SEQALIGN.C

```
/*
Program name: seqalign.c
Description: Concept of dynamic programming is
implemented in this program to calculate the score
for each element in the sequence matrix and print
it. The program uses swap to always put the maximum
length string in the array of sequential pointers.
Limitations:
```

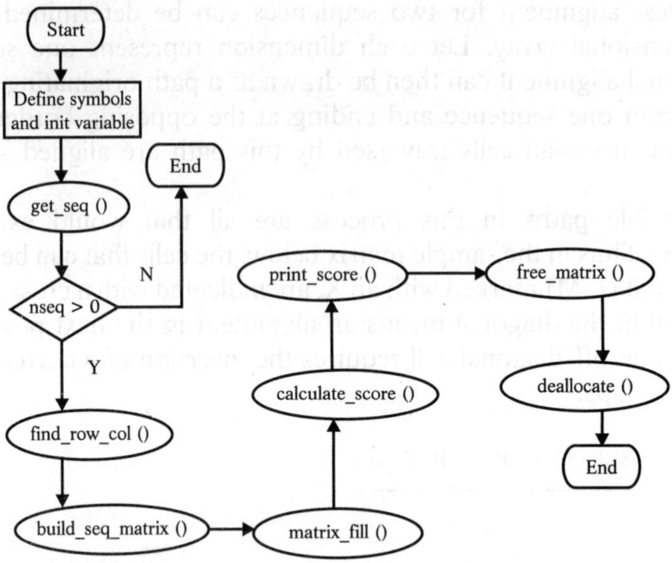

get_seq(): Gets sequences from the user; find_row_col(): Finds array dimensions from sequence lengths; build_seq_matrix(): Builds sequence matrix as per dimensions; matrix_fill(): Initialises the matrix with zeros or any predefined number; calculate_score(): Finds the max score of diag, left and above and fills the matrix locations with scores; print_score (): Prints matrix with scores calculated from sequence match, mismatch and gaps; free_matrix () and deallocate (): Releases all resources

Fig.11.5 Flow chart to compute scores

```
1. Maximum number of sequences is set to 2. Can be
changed to multiple sequences (a multiple of an even
number only).
2. Maximum sequence length is set to 20.
3. No trace back implementation for aligning
sequences is done.
 */

#include <stdio.h>
#include <stddef.h>
#include <malloc.h>
#define M_ROW 25 /* Maximum number of rows */
#define M_COL 25 /* Maximum number of columns */
#define M_SEQ_LEN 20 /* Maximum sequence length */
#define M_SEQ 2 /* Maximum number of sequences */
#define M 1 /* Sequence match score */
#define MM 0 /* Sequence mismatch score */
#define G 0 /* Gap */
```

```
#define INIT_VAL 0
#define SIZE (M_SEQ*M_SEQ_LEN) /* size of available
space */
#define swap(a, b) { temp=(a); (a)=(b);(b)=temp; }

static char sequence[SIZE]; /* storage for alloc */

int get_seq(char *seq_ptr[M_SEQ_LEN]);
void print_score(char*[],long, long);
int **build_seq_matrix(long, long, int);

void matrix_fill(char*[],long, long);
int validate_seq(char*);
void free_matrix(long, long);
void find_row_col(char* seq[], long* rc);
void calculate_score(char*[],long, long);
char *allocate_memory(int);
void deallocate_memory(char *);
int find_max(int, int, int);
void put_score(int i, int j, int match);

/* A pointer to an array of integer pointers or a
two-dimensional array */
int (*gbl_seq_matrix)[M_SEQ_LEN];
int **matrix_ptr;

main()
{
int i,result, nseq;
long rc[2]; /* holds the number of sequences */
char *seq[M_SEQ]; /* array of sequence pointers */

/* Gets the sequence list and the number of
sequences from the console */
seq[0]=(char *) malloc((size_t)((M_
SEQ)*sizeof(char)));
for(i=0;i<M_SEQ;i++) (*seq[i] = NULL);
nseq = get_seq(seq);
/* Exits from the program if there is no memory or
more than max seq count */
if (nseq == -1 ) exit(0);

find_row_col(&seq[0],&rc);
matrix_ptr = build_seq_matrix(rc[0],rc[1],nseq);
printf("\n No of rows %d\n", rc[0]);
printf("\n No of cols %d\n", rc[1]);
```

```
printf("\n\n");
matrix_fill(&seq[0],rc[0],rc[1]);
printf("\n\n");
 calculate_score(&seq[0],rc[0],rc[1]);
print_score(&seq[0],rc[0],rc[1]);

/* Free memory allocated */

free_matrix(rc[0],rc[1]);
deallocate_memory(seq);
}

int get_seq(char *seq_ptr[])
{
int i,nseq=0;
char *mem_ptr = 0; /* array of sequence pointer */
char input_seq[M_SEQ_LEN];
int seq_len = 0;

/* Gets the sequence list and the number of
sequences from the console */
printf("Enter the DNA sequence\n");
/* Gets the sequence from the user */
while ( nseq < M_SEQ)
{
if ( gets(input_seq)!= NULL)
  {
        seq_len = strlen(input_seq);
        if(!validate_seq(input_seq))
        {
              printf("Invalid SEQ \n");
              return(-1);
        }
        mem_ptr = allocate_memory(M_SEQ_LEN);
        if(!mem_ptr) return(-1);
        strcpy(mem_ptr,input_seq);
        seq_ptr[nseq++] = mem_ptr;

        printf("Enter the DNA sequence\n");
  }

}
for(i=0;i< M_SEQ;i++) printf("seq is %s\n", seq_
ptr[i]);
return(nseq);
}
```

```
void find_row_col(char* seq[],long* rc)
{
long nrow, ncol;
int i,j,seq_len[2];
/*Finds the sequence lengths for all the sequences
in the array of sequences*/
for(i=0; i<= M_SEQ; i++)
{
        seq_len[i] = strlen(seq[i]);
}
if ( seq_len[1]> seq_len[0] )
{
        ncol = seq_len[1] + 1;
        nrow = seq_len[0] +1;
}
else
{
  ncol = seq_len[0] +1;
  nrow = seq_len[1] +1;
}
*rc++ = nrow;
*rc = ncol;

return;
}

int validate_seq(char* s)
{
char *t;
t = s;
while (*t != '\0')
{
  *t = islower(*t) ? toupper(*t) : *t;
  if ( ((*t) == 'G') || ((*t) == 'A') || ((*t) ==
'C') || ((*t) == 'T'))
  {
  .     ++t;
  }
  else return (0);
}
return(1);
}

void calculate_score(char* seq[],long nrow, long
ncol)
{
```

```
/* define [i-1,j-1]:diag_pos,[i-1,j]:above_pos,[i,j-
1]:left_pos elements */
int diag_pos, above_pos,left_pos;
char *c_seq, *r_seq,rnt,cnt;     /* column sequence
and row sequence */
int i,j,max_pos;


/* Based on the sequence length, puts the max length
sequence in c_seq */

if( strlen(seq[0]) > nrow )
{
  c_seq = seq[0];   r_seq = seq[1];
}
else { c_seq = seq[1];    r_seq = seq[0]; }

for (i=1; i < nrow; i++)
{
    rnt = toupper(*r_seq);
    for (j=1; j < ncol; j++)
    {
              cnt = toupper(*c_seq);
        /* Compares all residues in the column
sequence against the current base in a row */
              if( rnt == cnt )
              {
                    put_score(i, j, M);
              }
              else
              {
put_score(i, j, MM);
              }


              if(!(*c_seq)) break; /* If no more
residues in the sequence then break */
              c_seq++;/* Moves to the next residue
in the sequence column */
        }
        c_seq -= (j-1);

        if (!(*r_seq)) break; /* Moves to the next
base in the sequence row */
    r_seq++;
}
r_seq -= (i-1);
```

```
return;
}

void put_score(int i, int j, int match)
{
int max_pos;
int diag_pos, above_pos,left_pos;

diag_pos = matrix_ptr[i-1][j-1] + match;
left_pos = matrix_ptr[i][j-1] + G;
above_pos = matrix_ptr[i-1][j]+G;
max_pos = find_max(diag_pos,left_pos,above_pos);
matrix_ptr[i][j] = max_pos;
}

int find_max(int diag_pos,int left_pos, int above_
pos)
{
if(diag_pos > left_pos)
{
  if(diag_pos > above_pos)
        return(diag_pos);
  else
        return(above_pos);
}
else
{
  if(left_pos > above_pos)
        return(left_pos);
  else
        return(above_pos);
}
}

void matrix_fill(char* seq[],long nrow, long ncol)
{
int i=0, j=0;
for (i=0; i < nrow; i++)

{
    for (j=0; j < ncol; j++)
    {
              if (i==0 || j==0) matrix_ptr[i][j] =
(int) 0;
              else matrix_ptr[i][j] = INIT_VAL;
```

```
                printf("%d\t",matrix_ptr[i][j]);
        }
      printf("\n");
    }
    return;
    }

    void print_score(char* seq[],long nrow, long ncol)
    {
    /* Sample seq1 is GAATTCAGTTA and Sample seq2 is
    GGATCGA */
    int i, j;
    char* c_base,*r_base;
    int** temp;

    if (strlen(seq[1]) > strlen(seq[0]) )
    {
      c_base = seq[1];
      r_base = seq[0];
    }
    else {
      c_base = seq[0];
      r_base = seq[1];
    }

    printf("\t");
    while ( (*c_base) != NULL)
    {
      if( islower(*c_base) ) printf("%c\t",toupper(*c_
    base) );
      else { printf("%c\t",*c_base);}
      c_base++;
    }
    printf("\n\n");

    for (i=0; i < nrow; i++)
    {
        for (j=0; j < ncol; j++)
        {
            printf("%d\t",matrix_ptr[i][j]);
             }

            if(i) {
                  if( islower(*r_base) ) printf("%c\
    t",toupper(*r_base++) );
                  else { printf("%c\t",*r_base++);}
```

```
        }
        printf("\n");

}
return;
}

/*
The row range is 0 to nrow-1 and column range 0 to
ncol-1
*/

int** build_seq_matrix(long nrow,long ncol,int nseq)
{
int **s;
int i;

/* allocate pointers to rows */
s=(int **) malloc((size_t)((nrow)*sizeof(int*)));
if (!s) printf("allocation failure\n");
s += 1;

/* Allocate rows and set pointers to them */
s[0]=(int *) malloc((size_t)((nrow*ncol)*sizeof(int)
));
if (!s[0]) printf("allocation failure\n");
s[0] +=1;

for(i=1;i<=nrow;i++) s[i]=s[i-1]+ncol;
/* return pointer to array of pointers to rows */
return(s);
}

void free_matrix(long nrow,long ncol)
{
int i;
free((char* ) (matrix_ptr[0])-1);
free((char* ) (matrix_ptr)-1);
}

static char *seqp = sequence; /* next free position
*/
char *allocate_memory(int n) /* return pointer to n
characters */
{
if (sequence + SIZE - seqp >= n) /* it fits */
```

```
{
  seqp += n;
  return seqp - n; /* old p */
}
else /* not enough room */
return 0;
}

void deallocate_memory(char *seq) /* free storage
pointed to by p */
{

if (seq >= sequence &seq < sequence + SIZE)
  seqp = seq;
}
```

OUTPUT

RUN 1

```
Enter the DNA sequence
atgc

Enter the DNA sequence
atgc

seq is ATGC
seq is ATGC

No of rows 5
No of cols 5

0  0  0  0  0
0  0  0  0  0
0  0  0  0  0
0  0  0  0  0
0  0  0  0  0

   A  T  G  C

0  0  0  0  0
0  1  1  1  1  A
0  1  2  2  2  T
0  1  2  3  3  G
0  1  2  3  4  C
```

RUN 2

```
Enter the DNA sequence
GAATTCAGTTA
Enter the DNA sequence
GGATCGA

seq is GAATTCAGTTA
seq is GGATCGA

No of rows 8
No of cols 12
```

INITIALISATION MATRIX WITH ZEROS

```
0  0  0  0  0  0  0  0  0  0  0  0
0  0  0  0  0  0  0  0  0  0  0  0
0  0  0  0  0  0  0  0  0  0  0  0
0  0  0  0  0  0  0  0  0  0  0  0
0  0  0  0  0  0  0  0  0  0  0  0
0  0  0  0  0  0  0  0  0  0  0  0
0  0  0  0  0  0  0  0  0  0  0  0
0  0  0  0  0  0  0  0  0  0  0  0
```

MATCH =1, MISMATCH = −1; GAP = 0

```
   G  A  A  T  T  C  A  G  T  T  A

0  0  0  0  0  0  0  0  0  0  0  0
0  1  1  1  1  1  1  1  1  1  1  1  G
0  1  1  1  1  1  1  1  2  2  2  2  G
0  1  2  2  2  2  2  2  2  2  2  3  A
0  1  2  2  3  3  3  3  3  3  3  3  T
0  1  2  2  3  3  4  4  4  4  4  4  C
0  1  2  2  3  3  4  4  5  5  5  5  G
0  1  2  3  3  3  4  5  5  5  5  6  A
```

MATCH =1, MISMATCH = 0; GAP = 0

```
   G  A  A  T  T  C  A  G  T  T  A

0  0  0  0  0  0  0  0  0  0  0  0
0  1  1  1  1  1  1  1  1  1  1  1  G
0  1  1  1  1  1  1  1  2  2  2  2  G
0  1  2  2  2  2  2  2  2  2  2  3  A
0  1  2  2  3  3  3  3  3  3  3  3  T
0  1  2  2  3  3  4  4  4  4  4  4  C
0  1  2  2  3  3  4  4  5  5  5  5  G
0  1  2  3  3  3  4  5  5  5  5  6  A
```

MULTIPLICATION OF PAM MATRICES

Bioinformatics uses a lot of algorithms which are matrix intensive. Therefore it is important for every bioinformatics student to learn the basics of matrix computation. In fact, Needleman and Wunsch dynamic programming and Smith–Waterman methodologies use matrix computation extensively. In this section we will introduce a matrix which will help to estimate the likelihood of change from one amino acid to another during short-term evolution—the PAM matrix. We will also discuss an algorithm for PAM matrix multiplication.

Point accepted mutation (PAM) matrix is a matrix calculated from comparing sequences with no more than 1% divergence. Scores are derived from the mutation probability matrix where each element gives the probability of AA (amino acid) in column (X) mutating to the AA in row (Y) after a particular evolutionary time, say for example after one PAM or 1% divergence. The alignment used in computing the PAM matrices is created from a limited set of closely related sequences. Multiplication of two PAM is also a PAM with the same characteristics but with different scores.

Let us consider PAM1 and PAM2 are the two matrices whose product has to be found. The product of PAM1 and PAM2 is stored in PAM3. Assume that PAM1 has m rows and n columns i.e. to say that the matrix has dimensions $m \times n$ and PAM2 has dimensions $n \times p$ (say) then PAM3 will have dimensions $m \times p$. Each row and column in a PAM matrix represents residue or amino acids.

GENERIC MATRIX MULTIPLICATION ALGORITHM IN C

Elements in matrices PAM1 and PAM3 are accessed row wise. The arrays and the dimensions of the arrays are passed to the function `pammul()`. The sequence arrays are treated as pointers during passing even though they are two-dimensional arrays. The same is applicable even if the array has more than two dimensions. The elements of the matrices PAM1 and PAM2 are manipulated using pointers within the function `pammul()`.

The generic matrix multiplication algorithm consists of three loops.

```
for i = 1 to m
{
  for j = 1 to p
   {
     PAM3ij= 0
   }
```

```
    for k = 1 to n
    {
            for j = 1 to p
            {
            PAM3ij= PAM3ij+ PAM1ik x PAM2kj
            }
    }
}
```

Let us illustrate the above algorithm using an example. Say PAM1 and PAM2 are 5 × 5 dimensional matrices.

$$PAM1 = \begin{array}{c} \\ A \\ R \\ N \\ D \\ C \end{array} \begin{array}{c} \begin{array}{ccccc} A & R & N & D & C \end{array} \\ \begin{pmatrix} 13 & 6 & 9 & 9 & 5 \\ 3 & 7 & 4 & 3 & 2 \\ 4 & 4 & 6 & 7 & 2 \\ 5 & 4 & 8 & 11 & 1 \\ 2 & 1 & 1 & 1 & 52 \end{pmatrix} \end{array}$$

$$PAM2 = \begin{array}{c} \\ A \\ R \\ N \\ D \\ C \end{array} \begin{array}{c} \begin{array}{ccccc} A & R & N & D & C \end{array} \\ \begin{pmatrix} 12 & 2 & 9 & 10 & 3 \\ 1 & 5 & 1 & 0 & 1 \\ 4 & 1 & 40 & 36 & 0 \\ 6 & 0 & 42 & 50 & 0 \\ 1 & 1 & 0 & 0 & 7 \end{pmatrix} \end{array}$$

Now PAM3 will be a 5 × 5 matrix filled initially with zeros. After the multiplication operation which will be explained, the resultant PAM3 will have the values shown below.

$$PAM3 = \begin{array}{c} \\ A \\ R \\ N \\ D \\ C \end{array} \begin{array}{c} \begin{array}{ccccc} A & R & N & D & C \end{array} \\ \begin{pmatrix} 257 & 70 & 861 & 904 & 80 \\ 079 & 47 & 320 & 324 & 30 \\ 120 & 36 & 574 & 606 & 30 \\ 163 & 39 & 831 & 888 & 26 \\ 87 & 62 & 101 & 106 & 371 \end{pmatrix} \end{array}$$

Multiplication process It is obvious from PAM1 and PAM2 that $m = 5$, $n = 5$ and $p = 5$. The first row elements in PAM1 = (13, 6, 9, 9, 5). The first column elements in PAM2 = (12, 1, 4, 6, 1). To compute the elements in the first row of PAM3, multiply the first row of matrix PAM1 with the first, second, third, fourth and fifth columns of matrix PAM2 as shown below.

```
The first element in the first row
= Sum of {(13, 6, 9, 9, 5) × (12, 1, 4, 6, 1)}
= 13 × 12 + 6 × 1 + 9 × 4 + 9 × 6 + 5 × 1 = 257
```

```
The second element in the first row
= Sum of {(13, 6, 9, 9, 5) × (2, 5, 1, 0, 1)}
= 13 × 2 + 6 × 5 + 9 ×1 + 9 × 0 + 5 × 1 = 70
The third element in the first row
= Sum of {(13, 6, 9, 9, 5) × (9, 1, 40, 42, 0)}
= 13 × 9 + 6 × 1 + 9 × 40 + 9 × 42 + 5 × 0 = 861
The fourth element in the first row
= Sum of {(13, 6, 9, 9, 5) × (10, 0, 36, 50, 0)}
= 13 × 10 + 6 × 0 + 9 × 36 + 9 × 50 + 5 × 0) = 904
The fifth element in the first row
= Sum of {(13, 6, 9, 9, 5) × (3, 1, 0, 0, 7)}
= 13 × 3 + 6 × 1 + 9 × 0 + 9 × 0 + 5 × 7 = 80
```

Therefore, the first row elements in PAM3 is (257, 70, 861, 904, 80) (Fig.11.6)

In a similar way, the elements of the second, third, fourth and fifth row of PAM3 can be computed.

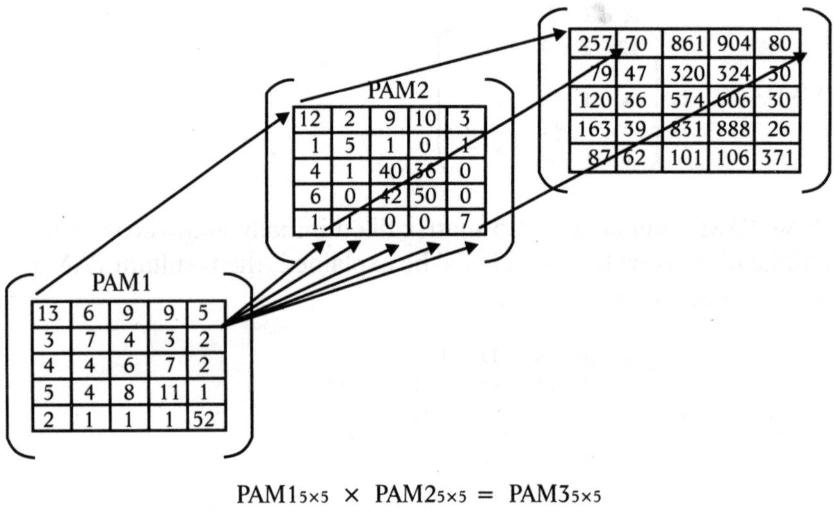

Fig.11.6 Multiplying matrix PAM1 with matrix PAM2

Implementation of matrix multiplication The program given below defines storage for three matrices, initialises two of them, and calls the matrix multiplication function `seqmul` to multiply them together. Note that the matrices are declared as simple two-dimensional integer arrays.

PROGRAM 11.2: PAM.C

```
/*
This program illustrates multiplication of two
matrices. The function pammul() multiplies two PAM
matrices and generates a third matrix with the
resultant values.
*/

#define R 5  /* row size of matrices PAM1 and PAM3*/
#define CR 5 /* row size of matrix PAM2 and column
size of matrix PAM1 */
#define C 5 /* column size of matrix PAM3 */

static int PAM1[R][CR]= { {13,6,9,9,5},
            {3,7,4,3,2},
                  {4,4,6,7,2},
         {5,4,8,11,1},
                  {2,1,1,1,52}
                };

static int PAM2[CR][C]= { {12,2,9,10,3},
                  {1,5,1,0,1},
                  {4,1,40,36,0},
         {6,0,42,50,0},
                  {1,1,0,0,7}
                    };
int PAM3[R][C];
void pammul(int, int, int,int*, int*, int*);
void print_pam(int row,int col,int *pam);

main()
{
print_pam(R,CR,&PAM1);
printf("\n\n\n");
print_pam(CR,C,&PAM2);
printf("\n\n\n");

pammul(R, CR, C, &PAM1, &PAM2, &PAM3);
printf("\n\n\n");
print_pam(R,C,&PAM3);
}

/* Prints matrix elements using row and column
dimensions */
```

```
void print_pam(int row,int col,int *pam)
{
int count,nelements,*ppam;
nelements = row*col;

count = 0;
ppam = pam;
while (nelements--)
{
  count++;
  printf ("%2d\t",*ppam++);
  if(count == col) { printf("\n"); count = 0;}
}
}
/* Multiply two input matrices using generic matrix
multiplication algorithm. m1r is the row dimension
of pam1,m2cr is the row dimension of pam2. m3c is
the column dimension of pam3*/

void pammul(int m1r, int m2cr, int m3c,int *pm1, int
*pm2, int *pm3)
{

int *pPAM2, *pPAM3;
int row,col,cr; /* no of rows , no of cols , col-row
dimension */
int nelements; /* total number of elements in PAM3
*/
nelements = m1r*m3c;
pPAM3 = pm3;

/* Initialise all the elements in the matrix PAM3
with zeros till nelements becomes zero */
while (nelements--)
*pPAM3++ = 0;

/* The loop runs for 5 iterations. As per algorithm
row = i */
row = m1r;
while (row--)
{
pPAM2 = pm2;
cr = m2cr;
/* The loop runs for 5 iterations. As per algorithm
cr = k */
while (cr--)
```

```
{
  pPAM3 = pm3;
  col = m3c;
  /* Multiply the PAM1 row elements with each PAM2
column elements and put it in the first row of PAM3
i.e. PAM3ij = PAM3ij + PAM1ik × PAM2kj
The max value of col is 5. As per algorithm col = j
  */
  while (col--)
  *pPAM3++ += ((*pm1) * (*pPAM2++));
  pm1++;
  } /* end of cr loop */
   pm3 += m3c;
  } /* end of row loop */
} /* end of the function */
```

OUTPUT

```
 13     6     9     9     5
  3     7     4     3     2
  4     4     6     7     2
  5     4     8    11     1
  2     1     1     1    52

 12     2     9    10     3
  1     5     1     0     1
  4     1    40    36     0
  6     0    42    50     0
  1     1     0     0     7

257    70   861   904    80
 79    47   320   324    30
120    36   574   606    30
163    39   831   888    26
 87    62   101   106   371
```

ANALYSIS OF PROMOTER SEQUENCE

In biology, a *promoter* is a region or site on the DNA situated upstream to a coding sequence. It controls gene transcription with the help of certain elements present in them called *transcription factors*. RNA polymerase, the enzyme which synthesises RNA, binds to these elements and initiates transcription. Since the location of promoters are usually just next to the coding, designating the positions in the promoter are done relative to the position where transcription of RNA begins for a particular gene (i.e., positions upstream are negative numbers counting back from –1, for example –100 is a position 100 base pairs upstream). The position where transcription begins is called the *transcription start site*.

The elements of a promoter include:

1. The transcription start site (TSS)
2. The downstream element
3. The TATA box (consensus sequence TATAAA, usually –25 bp upstream of TSS).
4. Upstream elements: GC box (consensus sequence GGGCGG, CCGCCC, usually –80 to –105 bp upstream from TSS), CAAT box (consensus sequence CCAAT, usually upstream to TATA box).

A large and varied number of algorithms have been developed to help detect promoters in genomic sequences. This is because promoter prediction is the basis of many gene prediction techniques. Also, in order to analyse a given sequence, we can generate a map of its promoter boxes with their relative and absolute positions for each occurrence. The sequence can then be generated at each occurrence from its absolute position in a separate output file.

The program given below will generate the map and the output file. It can be invoked using the command prompt

```
>proseq <seqfile>
```

PROGRAM 11.3: PROSEQ.C

```
/* The program works with following limitations:
1. The maximum sequence length is set to 4000 bases.
2. The maximum number of occurrences of a promoter
   within a sequence is set to 60.
3. The number of promoter boxes to search within a
   sequence is set to 5.
*/

#include <stdio.h>
#include <string.h>
#define TRUE 1
#define FALSE 0
#define MAXBASE 4000
#define MAX_OCCURENCE 60
#define MAXPROMOTERS 5
#define ARRSIZE (MAX_OCCURENCE*MAXPROMOTERS)
#define SEQPRO "seq.pro"
#define LOGSEQ "analysis.pro"
```

```
#define TEMPPRO "temp.pro"

struct proseq {
int pos[ARRSIZE];
int occurrence[MAXPROMOTERS];
int distance[MAXPROMOTERS][MAX_OCCURENCE];
int next_seq;
};
struct proseq *seq_p;

int find_pattern(char* begin, char* pattern[]);
int find_promoter(char *,char *,FILE*);
void printpromoters(char **pattern);
void seq_analysis(FILE*);
void seqgen(int,int,FILE *);
char* skip_header(char *seq, int seq_len, FILE *seq_
file);

static int seqno;
int header_len;

void main(argc,argv)
int argc;
char *argv[];
{
char prmtrseq[MAXBASE],fname[20],seq[133];
static char *pro_pattern[] = { "GGGCGG","CCGCCC","CC
AAT","TATAA","TATA"};
char    *s,*pseq,base;
int i = 0,offset,idx,match;
FILE *seq_fp, *pro_fp,*temp_fp;

if(argc <2)
{
  printf("Usage: compare <filename>\n");
  exit(0);
}
strcpy(fname,argv[1]);
printf("file name %s\n",fname);

/* Opens input and output sequence files */

if ( (seq_fp = fopen(fname,"r")) == NULL)
{
  printf( "The file %s cannot be opened\n",fname );
  exit(0);
```

```
}
else {printf( "The file %s is opened\n",fname ); }

if ( (pro_fp = fopen(SEQPRO,"w")) == NULL)
{
  printf( "The file %s cannot be opened\n",SEQPRO );
  exit(0);
}
else {printf( "The file %s is opened\n",SEQPRO ); }

if ( (temp_fp = fopen(TEMPPRO,"w")) == NULL)
{
  printf( "The file %s cannot be opened\n",TEMPPRO );
  exit(0);
}

memset( prmtrseq, '\0',(size_t)MAXBASE);
seq_p = (struct proseq *) malloc(sizeof(struct
proseq));
if(seq_p == NULL)
{
  printf("\nNo Memory available error\n");
  exit(0);
}

s = skip_header(seq,132,seq_fp);
if(s == NULL)
{
   printf("\nFile with no sequences\n");
   exit(0);
}

/* Get all the bases from the input sequence file and
put in prmtrseq storage */

fseek(seq_fp,(long)header_len,SEEK_SET);
while(!feof(seq_fp)) {
  base = getc(seq_fp);
  if(base == '\n') continue;
  prmtrseq[i++] = toupper(base);
  /*continue; */
}
prmtrseq[i] = '\0';
printf("promoter sequence data is \n\n");
printf("%s",pseq); */
```

```
fwrite( pseq, sizeof(char),strlen(pseq) , temp_fp );
fclose(temp_fp);
idx=0;

/* Find the number of occurrences for each promoter
and generate sequences for each occurrence */
for(i=0;i<MAXPROMOTERS;i++)
{
  pseq = &prmtrseq[0];
  offset = 0;
  seq_p->occurence[i]=0;

  do {

        fprintf(pro_fp,"\n\n Promoter to search :
%s\n",pro_pattern[i]);
        /* Finds the ith promoter in the sequence.
find_promoter returns the position of the promoter in
the sequence */
        offset = find_promoter(pseq,pro_
pattern[i],pro_fp);
        seq_p->pos[idx++] = offset;
        seq_p->occurence[i]++;
        pseq = pseq+offset;

  }while(offset>0);
  --idx;
  seq_p->occurence[i] -= 1;

}
printpromoters(pro_pattern);
seq_analysis(seq_fp);
fclose(seq_fp);
fclose(pro_fp);
free(seq_p);
}

void seq_analysis(FILE* seq_fp)
{
int pos,idx,nextpos,i;
char ans = 'N';

printf("\n Do You need an analysis <Press Y or N>\
n");
fflush(stdin);
```

```
scanf("%c",&ans);
if( toupper(ans) == 'Y')
{
  printf("\nEnter ABS value of the promoter\n");
  scanf("%d",&pos);
  for(i=0;i<MAXPROMOTERS;i++)
  {
        for(idx=0;idx<seq_p->occurence[i]; idx++)
        {
              if(seq_p->distance[i][idx] == pos)
              {
                    if(seq_p->occurence[i] <= 1)
nextpos = pos;
                    else nextpos =seq_p-
>distance[i][idx+1];
                    printf("\nNext promoter is at =
%d\n",nextpos);
                    seqgen(pos,nextpos,seq_fp);
              }
              else continue;
        }
  }
}
}

void seqgen(int pos,int nextpos,FILE* seq_fp)
{
FILE *log_fp,*temp_fp;
int result,len,i=0;
char seq[MAXBASE],base;

if ( (log_fp = fopen(LOGSEQ,"w")) == NULL)
{
  printf( "The file %s cannot be opened\n",LOGSEQ );
  exit(0);
}
else {printf( "\nThe file %s is opened for output
\n",LOGSEQ ); }

if ( (temp_fp = fopen(TEMPPRO,"r")) == NULL)
{
  printf( "The file %s cannot be opened\n",TEMPPRO );
  exit(0);
}
```

```
if(pos < 0) pos = 0;
if (pos> nextpos) nextpos=pos;
len = nextpos - pos;
result = fseek(temp_fp,(long)pos-1,SEEK_SET);
if( result )
{
 printf( "Error in accessing sequences %s", LOGSEQ);
   exit(0);
}
else
{
   printf("\nLength of the sequence %d\n",len);
   memset(seq,'\0',(size_t)MAXBASE);
   do {
          base = getc(temp_fp);
          seq[i++] = toupper(base);
          continue;
  }while(len-- !=1);
          printf( "%s", &seq[0] );
          fprintf(log_fp,"%s\n",seq);
}
fclose(log_fp);
fclose(temp_fp);
}

void printpromoters(char **pattern)
{
int i,p,idx,rel,abs;
printf("\n-----------------------------------\n");
printf("Promoter \t Repeat count \t Rel.distance \t
Abs distance\n");
printf("-----------------------------------\n");
idx=0;
for(i=0;i<MAXPROMOTERS;i++)
{

  for(p=0;p<seq_p->occurence[i]; p++)
  {
         if ( p==0)
         {
                rel = 0;
                abs = seq_p->pos[idx++];
                seq_p->distance[i][p] = abs;
         }
         else
         {
```

```
                rel = seq_p->pos[idx++];
                abs = abs+rel;
                seq_p->distance[i][p] = abs;
            }
            printf("%s \t\t %d\t\t %d\t\t %d\
n",pattern[i],seq_p->occurrence[i],rel,abs);
    }
    /*printf("array index = %d\n",idx);*/
}
}

int find_promoter(char *seq,char *promo,FILE *pfp)
{
char *found,retseq[MAXBASE],*t_found;
static int pos;

if(( found = strstr(seq,promo)) != NULL)
{
        if(!stricmp(promo,"TATA"))
        {
              if(toupper(*(found+4)) == 'A')
              {
                    /*printf("Inside TATA comp %s\
n",promo);*/
                    pos = (int)(found - seq + 1);
                    found = strstr(seq+pos,promo);
                    if(found == NULL) return(0);
              }
        }
        pos = (int)(found - seq + 1);
        fprintf(pfp,"\nDistance in the sequence :
%d\n",pos);
        fprintf(pfp,"\n %s \n\n","Sequence :");
              fprintf(pfp,"%s",found);
        return(pos);
}
else return(0);
}

char* skip_header(seq, seq_len, seq_file)
char *seq;
int seq_len;
FILE *seq_file;
{
char *s;
```

```
/* Read each line of the sequence input file till
seq_len or newline */
s = fgets(seq, seq_len, seq_file);
if (s == NULL) return(NULL);
 if(strchr(seq, '>'))
 {
    header_len = strlen(seq);
 }
return(s);
}
```

OUTPUT

```
file name testseq1.txt
The file testseq1.txt is opened
The file seq.pro is opened
```

Promoter	Repeat count	Rel.distance	Abs distance
CCGCCC	2	0	822
CCGCCC	2	22	844
CCAAT	2	0	548
CCAAT	2	198	746
TATAA	4	0	22
TATAA	4	532	554
TATAA	4	125	679
TATAA	4	208	887
TATA	21	0	72
TATA	21	54	126
TATA	21	36	162
TATA	21	70	232
TATA	21	91	323
TATA	21	21	344
TATA	21	171	515
TATA	21	57	572
TATA	21	2	574
TATA	21	20	594
TATA	21	80	674
TATA	21	201	875
TATA	21	74	949
TATA	21	25	974
TATA	21	23	997
TATA	21	22	1019

[1] Refer to Appendix to see testseq1.txt in detail.

```
TATA            21              22          1041
TATA            21              23          1064
TATA            21              22          1086
TATA            21              67          1153
TATA            21              12          1165

Do you need an analysis <Press Y or N>
Y

Enter ABS value of the promoter
162

Next promoter is at = 232

The file analysis.pro is opened for output

Lengh of the sequence 70
TATAGTAAGTCATATTCAATCAAGCACACTAAATCTCGTATTCTCCTGT
CTCTCTCTACCACACTATGCA
```

OUTPUT FILES

1. **seq.pro** It contains the dump of the sequences for each promoter box for all occurrences. The sequence for the first occurrence is extracted from the absolute distance and for all other instances from the relative position of the first.
2. **analysis.pro** It contains sequences extracted between two consecutive occurrences based on the user selection for a promoter box.
3. **temp.pro** It contains the dump of the original sequence but with no new line and carriage returns.

Appendix

Header Files

The dna.h that has been used in many programs in this book is shown below.

```
struct dna
{
char organism[10]; /* species type */
int purines; /* AG together called purines in a
given dna sequence - total count*/
int pyramidines; /* TC together called pyrimidines
in a given dna sequence*/
int seq_number; /* number of sequences */
int tata; /* promoter binding site */
};

/*char rpents[10]; receipients of blood type
char donars[10];donars of blood type */

struct bg
{
char btype; /* blood type */
char ab;
char ag; /* antibodies produced and antigens present
in the blood type */
};

struct human
{
struct dna insulin;
struct bg *bgrp;
```

```
char bloodgrp;
char race;
};

typedef struct {
int maxr, maxc;
int m [2][2];
} matrix;

struct protein
{
char aa_type; /* aa - amino acid abbrevations */
int mass; /* daltons */
float pka; /* pka COOH gp < 3 */
int occurance_in_ptns; /* % < 10 */
};
```

FASTA FILES

The sequence data files that have been used in most of the programs are given below.

DNA SEQUENCE FILE

```
>gi|124376423|gb|BC132432.1| Mus musculus carbonic
anhydrase 1, mRNA (cDNA clone MGC:164063
IMAGE:40130709), complete cds
CCAGCATCTTCTCTGAAGCTGAATCACAACCTAAATAAGAGAAAATGGCAAG
TGCAGACTGGGGATATGG
AAGCGAAAATGGTCCTGACCAATGGAGCAAGCTGTATCCCATTGCCAATGGA
AACAACCAGTCTCCTATT
GATATTAAAACCAGTGAAGCCAATCATGACTCCTCTCTGAAACCACTCAGCA
TCTCCTATAATCCTGCAA
CTGCCAAAGAAATTGTTAACGTGGGACATTCTTTCCATGTAATTTTTGATGA
CAGTAGCAACCAATCTGT
TCTGAAAGGTGGCCCTCTTGCTGATAGCTATCGGCTCACTCAGTTCCATTTT
CACTGGGGCAACTCAAAC
GACCATGGCTCTGAGCACACCGTGGATGGAACTAGATATTCTGGAGAGCTTC
ACTTAGTTCACTGGAATT
CTGCAAAGTACTCCAGTGCTTCTGAAGCCATCTCCAAGGCTGATGGCCTGGC
AATCCTTGGCGTTTTGAT
GAAGGTTGGTCCAGCCAACCCAAGCCTGCAGAAAGTACTTGATGCTCTAAAC
TCAGTTAAAACTAAGGGA
AAACGAGCCCCATTCACAAATTTTGACCCATCCAGTCTGCTTCCTTCATCTC
TGGATTACTGGACCTACT
TTGGCTCTCTGACTCACCCTCCTCTTCATGAAAGTGTGACCTGGGTGATCTG
CAAGGATAGCATCAGTCT
```

AAGCCCAGAGCAGCTGGCCCAGCTCCGTGGTCTTCTGTCAAGTGCAGAGGGA
GAGCCTGCAGTTCCAGTT
CTGAGCAACCACCGTCCACCCCAACCCCTGAAGGGCAGAACAGTCAGAGCCT
CATTTTGAGTCCCAGCAA
GGAATGAGTCCTCAATTAGGACCTGGCCCCCTCTACA

>gi|24663184|ref|NM_140298.2| Drosophila melanogaster Carbonic anhydrase 2 CG6906-RA (CAH2), mRNA
TAACCGCAGTTGTGTGACCGCGTTCGGCGGTGAGCACGGATAGTAAGACAG
TGTCTCCACTGTCAGCTT
AAAACCGTTCGAAAGCCACTAGATTTGTGTGCCCCAGTGCCGCAAATAGTTA
CAGTTCGTAAATTAGTCG
CGACTGGTGACAGTGCCCAGTAATTCCCGATAAGGGCAAGTGTGTTCCGTGA
AAAGTGAGTCCGCGGCAA
GGTGAAACCATGAGGAGGTGTCGCAACACCCCGTTCGCAATTGTCATTGCTC
CGATCTTGATTTGTGCTT
CTTTGGTCTTGGCCCAAGATTTTGGCTACGAGGGCAGACATGGACCCGAGCA
CTGGAGCGAGGATTACGC
CCGCTGCAGTGGAAAGCACCAGAGTCCCATAAACATCGACCAGGTCAGCGCC
GTGGAGAAGAAGTTTCCC
AAGCTGGAGTTTTTCAATTTCAAAGTGGTGCCCGACAATCTTCAAATGACGA
ACAACGGTCACACGGTGC
TGGTGAAGATGAGCTACAACGAGGACGAGATCCCAAGTGTGCGTGGTGGTCC
TTTGGCGGAGAAAACTCC
TCTGGGCTATCAGTTCGAACAGTTCCACTTTCACTGGGGCGAGAACGATACG
ATTGGCAGTGAGGATTTG
ATCAACAATCGTGCCTATCCCGCCGAGTTGCACGTGGTATTGCGGAATCTAG
AGTATCCGGACTTTGCCA
GCGCCCTGGACAAGGATCACGGCATCGCCGTGATGGCCTTCTTCTTTCAGGT
GGGCGACAAATCAACTGG
TGGCTATGAGGGCTTCACCAACTTGCTCTCCCAGATTGACCGCAAAGGCAAG
AGCGTTAATATGACCAAT
CCACTTCCACTGGGCGAGTACATCTCGAAGTCCGTGGAGAGTTACTTTAGCT
ACACTGGTTCTCTGACCA
CACCGCCTTGCAGTGAGGAGGTCACCTGGATTGATTTCACAACGCCCATTGA
CATCACGGAGAAGCAGTT
GAATGCCTTCCGTCTGCTGACAGCCAACGATGATCATCTGAAGAACAATTTC
CGACCCATCCAGCCGCTG
AACGATCGCACCTTGTACAAGAACTACATAGAAATTCCGATTCACAACATGG
GCTCGATTCCACTCGTCG
ATGCGGAAAATGCGGCTGGCAAGTGGAGGGCACAAGCCGCAGCAGTGCTGTT
GCCCCTCGTTGTCCTCGC
TGCATTGTCAAGGACCTCCATTTTCCGGGGTTTTTAATTAGAGTTCTGCGGT
GGTAAATCGAAGGTTAAA
TCGTTAAATGCCTAGCTGGCGCTTAGGCGTCCAATTAAGCGCTGTAATTTAC

```
ATTTTCCGCTCTTGTTCG
CCGTCGCTGTTTGTTGTTCAAACACGAGTCCCGGTAATTTCCTTCGGCAAGG
ACTCAACTGCCGTCAGGA
CATCCATTCATATCCACACACACACACATATATATATATATATAAATATATA
TATATGGGCAAACAAACA
GGCGGACGGTGGGCGAAATTATTAAACCCCAAATGGGCGGAGCTTCAGCTGG
CACGAAACCCTTACTCAT
CAATTATGCAGCACCTCGCACAGCGACTGTCAACCGAATCGTACCCCGTATC
CGTACCCGTTCCCGTACC
CGTACCCGTTCCCGTACCCGTAACCGTATCCGTATCCGTATCCCCATATTCC
CTTCCGTCCGAGGAGGCC
CGCCAGTGCGAGGGGAACCCCCTGGATGTCCTCGCTATTGCACATTGTGATT
TTAAATGCTTGGCACAAG
CAGAGCTTTTTATTCGTGTACCTTAGATTTAAGTTTTGTAAACATAAAACCG
TAATAAATTTTATTGTTT
AACATCTCATAAAGG

>gi|159477294|ref|XM_001696694.1| Chlamydomonas
reinhardtii gamma carbonic anhydrase (CAG3) mRNA,
complete cds
CGTGCAGTAGGCAGTTAGTCCATGCGAATCGTCTGGCCTTGTGCGGGGCTTT
CTACGTGACACAAGGATT
TAGGCCCTGAGTGCCCGATAGCTTTGCCCCAAAGCGGTGGACCATGTCGCTA
TTCAAGTCTAGCCTGCCT
GCGGGCTTCCTATTCCCCTATCGGCACCCCAAGGCCAAGGGGCTTGTTGAGG
GCACGCTTTATGGACTGG
GCTCCCTGTTTCGCGGCGTGGGCGCCGCGCTGGATGAGCTGGGCTCTATGGT
TCAGGGCCCTCAGGGTAG
TGTCAAGGACCACGTCCAGCCTAACCTGGCGTTTGCACCAGTGCACCGCAAG
CCGGATGTGCCCGTTAAC
GCGGGCCAGGTGGTGCCCGCTCCACCCGCTGCTGCTCGCACGCTGAAAATCA
AGGAGGTGGTTGTGCCCA
ACAAGCACAGCACCGCGTTCGTGGCTGCCAACGCCAATGTGCTCGGGAACGT
TAAGCTGGGGGCGGGCTC
ATCGGTGTGGTATGGCGCCGTGCTGCGCGGTGACGTGAACGGCATTGAGGTG
GGCGCCAACAGCAACATC
CAGGACAACGCCATCGTGCACGTGTCCAAGTACAGCATGGACGGCACGGCAC
GGCCCACCGTCATCGGCA
ACAATGTGACCATTGGCCACGCCGCCACGGTGCACGCCTGCACCATTGAGGA
CAACTGCCTGGTGGGCAT
GGGCGCCACCGTGCTCGACGGAGCGACGGTCAAGAGCGGCTCCATCGTGGCT
GCCGGCGCCGTGGTGCCG
CCCAACACCACCATCCCCTCGGGCCAGGTGTGGGCCGGCTCGCCCGCCAAGT
TCCTGCGCCACCTGGAGC
CGGAGGAGGCCAGCTTCATCGGCAAGTCTGCCAGCTGCTACGCCGAGCTGTC
CGCCATCCACAAGTTCGA
```

```
GCAGAGCAAGACGTTTGAGGAGCAGTACACGGAGAGCTGCATCATCAAGGAC
CGCGCCGCTCTGGCCGAC
CCGTCAAACTCAGTGCACCAGATGTGGGAGTACGACAGCCAGACGGCGTTGG
TGGCCCGCGCCAAGAGGT
AGAGAGAGGAGCTGCAAGGGCTGCTGCGGTAGGCATGCACTGCAGGCAGGCA
GGGTTGCCATGGCAGCAG
TCGAGGTGAACGACACGCGCGTAGGCTGTCATGCGTTCGGCGTTGAATGAGT
ACGGTGCACCGCACCAAC
AGCGGCTAATTAAAGTAGCGGAAGTATAGTTGAGACAACCACAGATTTAAGT
AATGTAGCGTCAATGTAC
CGTGGGGCATGGGCGCCCCAAACCTATTTAAATGACTCCCTATCTC
```

EMBL FASTA FILE

```
sequence1
SQ  Sequence 142 BP; 41 A; 32 C; 38 G; 31 T; 0 other;
    agcagcagga agcactatgg gcgcagcgtc aataacgctg
    acggtacagg ccagacaatt      60
    attgtctggt atagtgcaac agcaaaacaa tttgctgagg
    gctattgatg cgcaacagct      120
    tctgttgcaa ctcacagtct gg  142
//
sequence2
SQ  Sequence 141 BP; 42 A; 31 C; 37 G; 31 T; 0 other;
    gcagcaggaa gcactatggg cgcagcgtca ataacgctga
    cggtacaggc caaacaaata      60
    ttgtctggta tagtgaatca gccaaacaat ttgctgaggg
    ctattgaggc gcaacatatt      120
    ctgttgcaac tcacagtctg g   141
//
```

OTHER FILES USED

```
sequence1
SQ  Sequence 142 BP; 41 A; 32 C; 38 G; 31 T; 0 other;
    gtgctgcacg
//
sequence2
SQ  Sequence 141 BP; 42 A; 31 C; 37 G; 31 T; 0 other;
    acgctgcacg
//
sequence3
SQ  Sequence 142 BP; 41 A; 32 C; 38 G; 31 T; 0 other;
    gtgctgcacg
//
sequence4
SQ  Sequence 142 BP; 41 A; 32 C; 38 G; 31 T; 0 other;
```

```
gtatcacacg
//
```

PROMOTER SEQUENCE FILE

```
>I192_CCR2_M13Rev sequence exported from
I192_CCR2_M13Rev.scf
CCTACCCTCCATGTCAGTCACTATAACTATGTCACTCATGCACACTGTGCCC
AGAGTCAC
GCAACTCACTCTATATCCACGTTTCACATAAATATGCATCATCAGAGTAGTC
TCAGTTGT
GTCTCTATATCATGCACTTTCTATCTTCTCATCATCATCCATATAGTAAGTC
ATATTCAA
TCAAGCACACTAAATCTCGTATTCTCCTGTCTCTCTCTACCACACTATGCAT
ATACGGAT
TGCTAGTCTCTCTCTCGATACTGCACGGCACATACAGCTTAGAATAAATCAT
TAGGGAGA
TGCAGTGAGAGAGTAAGTACACTATACATCATCTAGCTGTTACTATATTGTC
ACATTCGT
GTTTTTCCATCTGTGCGTGCTATGCATACTCGACATATCGTCTCAGTATCTC
TCATACAT
AGCGCCTGTTGCTACTTCATATTCATCACACACACGACACTATTAGCAGAGC
GTACAGCG
CAGAAACAATATCTCCGATACATAATGCTGTCACTATATCTAACGTGATACA
TCGTGCCG
TGATATGCCAATGTATAAATCTCATAGATGGTATATAGATTGATATGATGAT
GTATACAT
TAATGTAGAATCAAGACCACTCATTATCTTACTTAACACTTACAGCTTAATC
AAATTTAT
TAATTAATTCAGATATACTATAAAAATAGCTAGAGGTTTTAACATCCTTTAC
CATCGCCC
AAGTCCACGGATGACACACTTGGCACCAATATCCCACCCCGCCGCGCACCGT
ATTAGCGC
TCTGTCCCCTTTCTCCCTTTTCCTACCCGCCTCCGCTCCTCCCGCCCCCTTG
TCGGCCTC
ACCCCGCCCCAGCCTTCCCCTTTCCAGACTGCCTTATAGTGAGTAGTATAAC
ACAGCCCA
TTTTTAGTCGTACTACATGGCCCTTTAGTGAGTCGTATTACACGGCCCTATA
GTGAGTGG
TATTACACGGCCCTATAGTGAGTCGT ATTACGCCCTATAGTGAGTCGTATT
ACGCCCTAT
AGTGAGTCGTATTACGCCCTATAGTGAGTCGTATTACGGCCCTATAGTGAGT
CGTATTAC
GCCCTATAGTGAGTCGTATTACAATCGGATCCCGGGCCCGTCGACTGCAGAG
GCCTGCAT
GCAAGCTTCCCTATAGTGAGTCGTATAGAGCGCG
```

BUILT-IN LIBRARY FUNCTIONS

The operating system provides the user many built-in functions that may be called from a C program. We will list here some of the most commonly used build-in functions along with their prototypes. The function prototypes are provided in the header files of the compiler. Consult the system documentation for the complete set of library functions that are supported by the system.

S.No	Function name	Function prototype	Description
1.	abs(n)	int abs(int)	Calculates the absolute value of n
2.	asctime (timeptr)	char* asctime(const struct tm *)	Converts time structure pointer timeptr to a character string
3.	atof(s)	double atof(const char *)	Converts string s to double
4.	atoi(s)	int atoi(const char *)	Converts string s to integer
5.	atol(s)	long atol(const char *)	Converts string s to long
6.	ctime (timeptr)	char *ctime(const time_t *)	Converts the time pointer by timeptr into string
7.	difftime (t1,t0)	double difftime (time_t, time_t)	Finds the difference between two times t1 and t0
8.	exit(status)	void exit(int)	Terminates the calling process with status code
9.	fclose(fp)	int fclose (FILE *)	Closes the file with file pointer fp
10.	fcloseall	int fcloseall(void)	
11.	feof(fp)	feof(FILE *)	Verifies if the file has reached the end of file

S.No	Function name	Function prototype	Description
12.	fflush(fp)	int fflush (FILE *)	Flushes data from buffers to file indicated by fp
13.	fgetc(fp)	int fgetc (FILE *)	Gets the next character from file pointed by fp
14.	fgets(b,n,fp)	char *fgets(char *, int, FILE *)	Reads n-1 characters or until new line is reached from file fp into buffer b
15.	fopen(fp,m)	FILE *fopen(const char *, const char *)	Opens the file with the permissible modes
16.	fprintf(fp, args..)	int fprintf (FILE *, const char *, ...)	Writes the specified arguments into the file indicated by fp
17.	fputc(c,fp)	int fputc(int, FILE *)	Writes character c into the file pointed by fp
18.	fputs(buf,fp)	int fputs(const char *, FILE *)	Writes characters contained in buf to the file pointed by fp
19.	fread(buf, size,n,fp)	size_t fread(void *, size_t, size_t, FILE *)	Reads n items of data from file pointed by fp. Length of each data item is size bytes
20.	free(pointer)	void free (void *)	Releases memory block pointed by the pointer
21.	fscanf(fp, format, args..)	int fscanf FILE *, const char *, ...)	Data items are read from file fp into arguments as per the format
22.	fseek(fp, offset,mode)	int fseek (FILE *, long, int)	The file fp is positioned for I/O as per the offset and mode

S.No	Function name	Function prototype	Description
23.	ftell(fp)	long ftell (FILE *)	Returns the current position of the file in terms of offset in bytes
24.	fwrite(buf, size,n,fp)	size_t fwrite(const void *, size_t, size_t, FILE *)	Writes n items of data to the file pointed by fp. Length of each data item is size bytes
25.	getc(fp)	int getc(FILE *)	Reads the next character from the file pointed by fp
26.	Getchar()	int getchar(void)	Reads the next character from the standard input (stdin)
27.	gets(buf)	char *gets (char *)	Reads into buf from stdin a stream of characters until new line is encountered
28.	isalpha(ch)	int isalpha (int)	Check if 'ch' is an alphabetic character
29.	isalnum(ch)	int isalnum (int)	Check if 'ch' is an alphanumeric character
30.	islower(ch)	int islower (int)	Check if 'ch' is lower case character
31.	isupper(ch)	int isupper (int)	Check if 'ch' is upper case character
32.	localtime (timeptr)	struct tm *localtime (const time_t *)	Converts the time value and corrects for local time zone
33.	malloc(size)	void *malloc(size_t)	Allocates contiguous memory of size bytes
34.	memset(buf, c, count)	void *memset (void *, int, size_t)	Initialises the buffer to the specified character 'c' for count bytes

S.No	Function name	Function prototype	Description
35.	perror(err)	void perror(const char *)	Print the error message string pointed by err
36.	printf (format, args..)	int printf (const char *, ...)	Writes the argument as per format to the standard output: stdout
37.	putc(ch)	int putc(int, FILE *)	Puts the character 'ch' into the file pointed by fp
38.	putchar(ch)	int putchar (int)	Puts the character 'ch' to the stdout
39.	puts(buf)	int puts(const char *)	Puts the characters from buf to stdout till a null is encountered
40.	rand	int rand(void)	Generates a pseudorandom number
41.	remove(path)	int remove (const char *)	Deletes a file found in the path
42.	rewind(fp)	void rewind (FILE *)	Resets the file to beginning position
43.	scanf(format, args...)	int scanf(const char *, ...)	Reads data into arguments from stdin as per format
44.	sprintf(buf, format, args...)	int sprintf (char *, const char *, ...)	Prints the arguments as per the format into the buffer (nothing but a character array)
45.	sqrt(x)	double sqrt(double)	Returns the square root of x
46.	sscanf(buf, format, args...)	int sscanf (const char *, const char *, ...)	Data is read from the buffer into the arguments as per the format
47.	strcat (s1,s2)	char *strcat(char *,const char *)	Concatenates two strings s1 and s2

S.No	Function name	Function prototype	Description
48.	strchr(s,c)	char *strchr(char*, char)	Search the first occurrence of a character c in a given string s
49.	strcmp (s1,s2)	int strcmp(const char *, const char *)	Compares strings s1 and s2
50.	strcpy (s1,s2)	char *strcpy(char *, const char *)	Copies the string s2 to s1
51.	strlen(s)	size_t strlen(const char *)	Find the number of characters in s excluding the null character
52.	strncmp(s1, s2,n)	int strncmp(const char *, const char *, size_t)	n characters of string s1 and s2 are compared
53.	strncpy(s1, s2,n)	char *strncpy (char *, const char *, size_t);	Copies n characters from s1 to s2
54.	strrchr(s,c)	char *strrchr (const char *, int)	Searches the string s for the last occurrence of c
55.	strstr (string, substring)	char *strstr (const char *, const char *)	Finds the sub string in string
56.	strtok (string, token)	char *strtok (char *, const char*)	Finds the next token in a string
57.	strtol (strptr, stoptr, base)	long strtol (const char *, char **, int);	Converts strings to a long integer value
58.	system	int system (const char *)	Runs a program in a shell
59.	tolower(a)	int tolower(int)	Returns the lower case of character a
60.	toupper(a)	int toupper(int)	Returns the upper case of character a

S.No	Function name	Function prototype	Description
61.	ungetc(ch, fp)	int ungetc(int, FILE *)	Puts back the character 'ch' into the file indicated by fp
62.	vprintf	int vprintf(FILE*, constchar *, ...)	
63.	time (timeptr)	time_t time(time_t *)	Gets the system time and stores it in the memory pointed by timeptr

ASCII TABLE

Decimal	Octal	Hex	Character
0	0	00	NUL
1	1	01	SOH
2	2	02	STX
3	3	03	ETX
4	4	04	EOT
5	5	05	ENQ
6	6	06	ACK
7	7	07	BEL
8	10	08	BS
9	11	09	HT
10	12	0A	LF
11	13	0B	VT
12	14	0C	FF
13	15	0D	CR
14	16	0E	SO
15	17	0F	SI
16	20	10	DLE
17	21	11	DC1
18	22	12	DC2
19	23	13	DC3

Decimal	Octal	Hex	Character
20	24	14	DC4
21	25	15	NAK
22	26	16	SYM
23	27	17	ETB
24	30	18	CAN
25	31	19	EM
26	32	1A	SUB
27	33	1B	ESC
28	34	1C	FS
29	35	1D	GS
30	36	1E	RS
31	37	1F	US
32	40	20	SP
33	41	21	!
34	42	22	"
35	43	23	#
36	44	24	$
37	45	25	%
38	46	26	&
39	47	27	'
40	50	28	(
41	51	29	)
42	52	2A	*
43	53	2B	+
44	54	2C	,
45	55	2D	-
46	56	2E	.
47	57	2F	/
48	60	30	0
49	61	31	1
50	62	32	2
51	63	33	3
52	64	34	4
53	65	35	5

Decimal	Octal	Hex	Character
54	66	36	6
55	67	37	7
56	70	38	8
57	71	39	9
58	72	3A	:
59	73	3B	;
60	74	3C	<
61	75	3D	=
62	76	3E	>
63	77	3F	?
64	100	40	@
65	101	41	A
66	102	42	B
67	103	43	C
68	104	44	D
69	105	45	E
70	106	46	F
71	107	47	G
72	110	48	H
73	111	49	I
74	112	4A	J
75	113	4B	K
76	114	4C	L
77	115	4D	M
78	116	4E	N
79	117	4F	O
80	120	50	P
81	121	51	Q
82	122	52	R
83	123	53	S
84	124	54	T
85	125	55	U
86	126	56	V
87	127	57	W

Decimal	Octal	Hex	Character
88	130	58	X
89	131	59	Y
90	132	5A	Z
91	133	5B	[
92	134	5C	\
93	135	5D	]
94	136	5E	^
95	137	5F	_
96	140	60	`
97	141	61	a
98	142	62	b
99	143	63	c
100	144	64	d
101	145	65	e
102	146	66	f
103	147	67	g
104	150	68	h
105	151	69	i
106	152	6A	j
107	153	6B	k
108	154	6C	l
109	155	6D	m
110	156	6E	n
111	157	6F	o
112	160	70	p
113	161	71	q
114	162	72	r
115	163	73	s
116	164	74	t
117	165	75	u
118	166	76	v
119	167	77	w
120	170	78	x
121	171	79	y

Decimal	Octal	Hex	Character
122	172	7A	z
123	173	7B	{
124	174	7C	|
125	175	7D	}
126	176	7E	~
127	177	7F	DEL

Index